Sale or
Succession?

If you want to know how...

Buying a Business and Making it Work
A step-by-step guide to purchasing a business and making it successful

This book takes you through the five essential phases that will help you to achieve your personal and professional objectives.

Turning a Business Around
How to spot the warning signs and ensure a business stays healthy

'Inspiring and full of proven steps to help you trade out of tough times.' – HSBC Business Update

Your Business, Your Pension
How you can use your business to provide for a better retirement

This book will help you to deal with the coming pensions crisis so you can provide a realistic income for your retirement.

Your Retirement Masterplan
How to ensure you have a fulfilling and enjoyable third age

'The most down to earth, common sense book on retirement I have ever read.' – BBC Radio Humberside

howtobooks
Send for a free copy of the latest catalogue to:
How To Books
3 Newtec Place, Magdalen Road,
Oxford OX4 1RE, United Kingdom
email: info@howtobooks.co.uk
http://www.howtobooks.co.uk

Sale or Succession?

John Hawkey

howto**books**

Published by How To Books Ltd,
3 Newtec Place, Magdalen Road,
Oxford, OX4 1RE, United Kingdom.
Tel: (01865) 793806. Fax: (01865) 248780.
email: info@howtobooks.co.uk
http://www.howtobooks.co.uk

British Library Cataloguing in Publication Data
A catalogue record for this book is available from
the British Library.

Produced for How To Books by Deer Park Productions, Tavistock
Prepared by *specialist* publishing services, Milton Keynes
Cover design by Baseline Arts, Oxford
Printed and bound by Bell & Bain Ltd, Glasgow

Note: The material contained in this book is set out in good faith for general
guidance and no liability can be accepted for loss or expense incurred as a
result of relying in particular circumstances on statements made in the book.
The laws and regulations are complex and liable to change, and readers
should check the current position with the relevant authorities before making
personal arrangements.

Contents

List of figures

Introduction

Every owner of a private business will have to exit his or her business one day. This is as inevitable as the certainty of death and taxes. Surely this means that the majority of small business owners have planned vigorously for this inevitability? Unfortunately, from my experience, it does not!

I have been involved in advising private business owners about exit planning for nearly 20 years. In this time two things, in particular, have struck me. First, that while most business owners accept, in theory, the need and the value of planning their business exit, very few actually do so. Secondly, that when they do plan, they do so far too late.

The failure to plan long-term arises, I believe, largely because of a fundamental misunderstanding of what exit planning is all about. This is best illustrated by the widely held notion that exit planning is analogous to painting your house before you sell it. In fact, nothing could be further from the truth. A last minute paint job is short-term, superficial and largely transparent, adding only marginally to a house's value and saleability. Exit planning is long-term, structural and fundamental and should significantly improve both the business's chances of sale and its value on sale.

My purpose in this book is to help business owners to understand the true nature of exit planning. I hope to convince those starting a new business venture that the key to success is to begin exit planning from the beginning, because it is then that many important aspects of exit planning (such as ownership structure and shareholders' agreements) are best settled.

For the owners of mature businesses, my message is: begin your planning immediately. However, I fear many of you will treat this message with some scepticism.

When asked how they rate the urgency of exit planning, the majority of owners respond that they will 'get around to it when they have to'. The fundamental flaw with this approach is that unexpected events or circumstances (such as the death of a business partner) can arise at any time, throwing all your plans into chaos. Unfortunately, the painful lesson to be learnt is that many such problems cannot be remedied after the event and that exit planning will not always wait until you are ready.

I also aim to explain to all business owners (be they start-up entrepreneurs, or experienced hard heads, or majority or minority shareholders) that exit planning is, fundamentally, a simple process that requires business common sense and a degree of application rather than sophisticated financial or legal expertise. Any competent business owner who is prepared to think ahead and take expert advice where necessary can undertake the task.

Finally, I would like to share with you a comment I heard recently:

> *'The best time to start planning your exit is from start-up.*
> *The next best time is now!'*

1

What do you want from your business?

This chapter is the beginning of your exit planning journey. You start by considering what you want from your business by answering a series of questions: this will help you establish your objectives. Next, you will consider how you can achieve these objectives. Your answers will, inevitably, lead you to think carefully about your exit.

We then consider answers I have received to similar questions I put to other business owners. We see from their answers that most consider wealth creation and independence to be their primary business objectives, although many are uncertain on how these are to be achieved.

We will then consider whether owning a business or working for someone else best achieves the objectives of wealth creation and independence.

Finally, we will summarise the steps involved in the exit-planning process.

ESTABLISHING YOUR OBJECTIVES

The philosopher Seneca said: 'When a man does not know which harbour he is heading for, no wind is the right wind.' John Lennon, 2000 years later, made much the same point when he asked: 'How can I go forward when I don't know which way I'm facing?'

Before you plan a journey you need to know where you want to go.

1

Similarly, before you start planning your exit, you should have a clear understanding of what you want from your business. Do you consider it as a source of income only; or do you think it will also provide you with a substantial capital sum on which to retire? Will you manage your business for life and close it down when you quit; or do you plan to pass it on to your son or daughter? In other words, what are your business objectives? You can establish this by asking yourself five questions, as follows:

1   Ask yourself: 'Why am I in business?' or, 'What do I want from my business?'

   If you are considering starting a business, ask yourself: 'Why do I want to go into business?' or: 'What do I want from my new business?'

   Write down your answers.

   Your answers should help you begin to focus on ambitions such as personal satisfaction, wealth creation and independence. You will note that most of these assume that you will dispose of your business for value one day. If wealth creation is prominent in your business objectives, you should think about how you will build the value of your business as well as how you will dispose of it.

2   Ask yourself: 'How much longer do I want to work in the business?' (In other words, when do you plan to exit?)

   Your answer will need to be consistent with your target exit value, which is considered next.

3   Now ask yourself: 'What do I think my business is worth now?' and

4   'What do I wish to get for my business when I exit?'

   These questions are important because you need to set your exit plans within the context of the current and expected values of your business and your financial requirements. For example, if you plan to retire after you sell, how much capital do you require and where will this come from? How much do you expect to get from the sale of your business to add to what you have already saved or accumulated in your pension fund?

   Also, is it reasonable to expect that your business will achieve its target exit value by the time of your planned exit date?

5   Lastly, ask yourself: 'How do I plan to leave my business?'

For example, do you plan to transfer it to an heir? Or sell it through a trade sale or, perhaps to your management? Have you considered franchising as an exit option? Is a flotation (or public listing) a possibility and, if so, what do you know about the various stock exchanges in the UK?

Where you plan to leave your business to an heir, have you considered how the heir will pay you for the business? Will this be in cash, or will it have to be on a deferred payment basis? If the payment is deferred (perhaps because the heir has no means of raising the total purchase), will the payment be sufficient to meet your needs? These same considerations could apply to a sale to your management and/or employees.

COLLATING YOUR ANSWERS

You can now collate your answers to get an (albeit preliminary) overview of your overall business objectives, which should be closely linked to your specific exit objectives. For example, your answers could be as follows:

1   I am in business because:
   • I wish to have an interesting and varied life;
   • I wish to build up enough money to retire comfortably.

2   I plan to exit my business when I am 55, that is in 8 years' time.

3   I believe my business is worth £350000 now and I plan to sell it for £500000.

4   I hope to sell the business to my senior management.

5   I believe my management will be able to pay me in cash by raising finance against the business's assets.

TEST YOUR ASSUMPTIONS

Having collated your objectives, test your assumptions by asking yourself the following questions:

- How realistic are your plans? Is your value target reasonable and is it based on both a real current value and achievable growth targets?
- Are your objectives consistent with each other? (Using our example, is it realistic here to assume that that your management will be able to raise the £500000 you hope to get for your business? Are there hard assets in the business that will make this borrowing possible?)
- Are you expecting to be paid in cash, or can you retire comfortably and receive payment over time?
- In reality (as opposed to the theory) is your business likely to be attractive to buyers at the price you are talking about? (To assist you in this, list three good reasons why someone would buy your business at the price you are asking.)
- And finally, how are you going to achieve your plans?

We can now compare your answers with those I have received from other business owners.

ANSWERS FROM OTHER BUSINESS OWNERS

QUESTION 1: WHAT DO YOU WANT FROM YOUR BUSINESS?

As you might expect, most business owners put 'making more money', or 'creating more wealth' (and variants thereof) high on their list, although 'being independent' was not too far behind. For many owners, independence meant financial independence, although for some independence in the sense of being your own boss and having the freedom to do what you want, was also important.

For owners with a business in which family members work or are intending to work, a major objective was to 'build up value for the family', or 'to pass on the business to my family'. This objective can be seen as a mixture of wealth creation and the desire to be a benefactor.

Most business owners are clear about their overall wealth-creation strategy, which is to start (or acquire) a business, build it up, sell it and retire on the proceeds. But for many, the strategy is vague when it comes to method and timescale for exit and the amount of capital that is necessary for a comfortable retirement.

For family business owners the strategy is similar in terms of building up the business, but the main objective is usually to pass on the business to heirs, with the exiting owner receiving some, but not necessarily all, of the capital value on retirement.

A summary of these answers is shown in Figure 1.1 below.

- To make more money.
- To build up enough wealth to retire in comfort.
- To be my own boss.
- To achieve independence.
- To achieve freedom.
- To create a business to pass on to my children.
- Because I was left the business by my father.
- To prove to myself that I could do it.
- To work in a business with my wife/husband/family.
- To commercialise my invention, my intellectual property or my ideas.
- To have a more interesting life.
- I am attracted to entrepreneurship and the idea of building up a business empire.
- I like the power of being the boss.
- To build it up, sell it and buy a bigger business.

Figure 1.1. Why am I in business?

QUESTION 2: WHEN DO YOU PLAN TO EXIT?

Most owners gave an answer based on their age, such as 'When I am 55.' The impression was that most had not really thought this through and were content to let things develop naturally and hoped that 'perhaps, something would come up'. A minority group, whose ambition was to buy and sell several businesses in their lifetime (known by some as 'serial entrepreneurs'), had a clearer idea of their exit timing, which was usually about five to eight years from acquisition. Finally, there were those who seemed content to stay in business to the end and had no time scale to exit at all (known as 'managers for life').

QUESTIONS 3 AND 4: WHAT IS THE VALUE OF YOUR BUSINESS?

An analysis of the answers reveals that most owners:

- had, at best, a vague idea of the current value of their busines;
- who did have a firm view, overestimated the value by basing it on unsubstantiated hopes rather than firm valuation principles;
- had little idea of what their business would be worth when they planned to sell;
- had no firm plans on how to grow business value to their target exit amount.

QUESTION 5: HOW DO YOU PLAN TO EXIT?

Most business owners had a limited view of the exit options that might be available to them. Family business owners were, naturally, usually focussed on a handover to a designated family member; whilst for those without families a trade sale was the favoured option. Others had considered a sale to management or employees. In most cases the merits of one exit option over another had not been thought through. Few owners had a plan B should their favoured exit option prove not to be feasible.

WHAT CAN WE LEARN FROM THE ANSWERS?

The first conclusion that can be drawn is that financial reward and independence are the most important business objectives for existing small to medium sized enterprise (SME) owners and those considering going into business. For family business owners, passing on something of value to heirs was a major objective.

How does this apply to you? If wealth creation and independence were also your primary objectives, do you think that you can create more real wealth through your business than you are likely to generate by working for someone else? Also, have you considered whether this increased reward will come from income generation, or building capital growth? If you have a family business, have you considered whether your designated heir will be capable of running a business and what steps you intend to take to prepare him or her for the task?

The second conclusion is that most owners have not sufficiently thought about *when* they will exit their businesses, leaving it to chance or fate, or believing that the decision can be made (or will become obvious) later on. When you gave your answer about the timing of your exit did this follow a carefully thought-out plan and is this part of your operational business plan? Have you considered whether your time target is likely to be a good period in which to sell with regard to market conditions in your industry?

The third conclusion is that most owners have an unrealistic idea of business values and have no firm plans to build the business to reach the target value they have hoped to achieve. Does this also apply to you? Have you based your answers on an up-to-date, formal valuation provided by a professional valuer, or your own estimates? If you have used your own estimates, what valuation methods have you used?

The last conclusion is that most business owners have a limited understanding of the range of exit options available to them and hence, in most cases, fall back on a trade sale 'to some interested party' (or a hand-over to a family member), without having analysed who the interested party would be (or whether the chosen family member is suitable, or even willing to take on the business). Also, without a clear exit option in mind, most of them have made no effort to tailor the growth and development of their business to the type of exit they believe is the optimum one.

How do you shape up here? Could some of these conclusions also apply to you? Have you got a plan, or do you fall into the large category of business owners described by John H. Brown in *Exit Planning Review* when he said:

> '… few owners reach their objectives. Why? Because they don't have a plan to achieve them.'

SHOULD YOU OWN A BUSINESS, OR GET A JOB?

It is clear from the responses of business owners that most consider wealth creation and independence to be their primary objectives. But, it is worth asking whether these objectives are achieved more easily through owning a business than they could be through working for someone else. Similarly, will you, as head of the family, create more wealth for your family by going into business than you could by being employed?

1) WEALTH CREATION

The most obvious difference between owning a business and having a job is that with a business you have the potential to create wealth in two ways, firstly by earning income and secondly by building capital value in the business.

With regard to income generation, the average small business owner probably earns less than an employee in a senior management role, either because he is putting back most of the profits into the business, or because profits are not large or predictable enough to allow for generous drawings. So, in most cases, if a business owner is to create greater wealth than an employee, it is necessary for him to build capital value in the business.

However, it is not enough just to create value in a business; it must also be converted into cash in the owner's pocket when he exits. For this to happen, there are two necessary steps involved, namely:

Step 1: Building the value in the business.
Step 2: Realising the value through a disposal of the business assets by the owner to a third party.

Because there is usually an element of deferred payment in a family succession, the family business owner usually requires four steps to achieve a successful succession, namely:

Step 1: Building business value.
Step 2: A completed transfer to the designated heir.
Step 3: The heir needs to be able to raise the cash to pay for the business.
Step 4: The heir needs to make a success of the business (to ensure the business survives and, if payment is on terms, that the owner gets paid).

(An important associated issue in a successful disposal is paying the least possible amount of tax and I will deal with this in detail in Chapter 10.)

2) A SUCCESSFUL DISPOSAL

Many business owners spend most of their time on the first step of creating value, but fail to spend enough time planning for the other steps. As I explain in this book, a successful exit requires thoughtful planning and implementation of all stages of the process. Without this, building theoretical capital wealth alone will be a fruitless exercise.

To achieve a successful disposal it is crucial that the business owner is not blocked by what I call a technical barrier to sale, which he has overlooked, or not foreseen. By way of example, consider the following circumstances.

A business owner, with a large majority shareholding, wishes to sell his business through a trade sale. The potential purchaser will pay the asking price, but only if he can purchase 100% (i.e. all the shares) of the business. The minority shareholder states he does not wish to sell his shares. There is no shareholders' agreement in place that compels the minority shareholder to sell his shares.

In these circumstances, the minority shareholder could cause the sale to fall through, or hold the majority shareholder to ransom by demanding a price for his shares in excess of the price that the owner will receive from the purchaser. Unfortunately, for majority shareholders without a shareholders' agreement, these circumstances are not uncommon.

(Shareholders' agreements are covered in more detail in Chapter 5.)

3) BEING INDEPENDENT

Whether or not independence *can* be achieved through owning a business is partly dependent on what sort of independence is being contemplated. Independence in the sense of the freedom (i.e. the time and the money) to do whatever you want is unusual for most small business owners during their period of ownership. It is largely a myth that owning a business leads to a freer, easier life than that enjoyed by most employees. In fact, for most small business owners the reverse is the case, as small business ownership involves long working hours and a great deal of stress and can often result in financial failure.

However, small business ownership *can* lead to financial independence and personal freedom once the owner has achieved a successful disposal (or transfer) of his business at the target price. It would seem obvious, therefore, that the rewards of a successful exit justify the efforts of careful exit planning and implementation.

THE EXIT PLANNING PROCESS

In the balance of this book you will read about how to plan for the successful exit of your business. However, I think it would be helpful at this stage to summarise the exit planning process. This is done in Figure 1.2, below.

1   Exit planning is not just about selling a business: it is about how to structure and prepare a business for disposal and, where applicable, how to groom the purchaser/s for the task of taking it over. This distinction is easy to grasp if you realise that exit planning is not an isolated event, but a long-term process.

2   Exit planning should not be undertaken in isolation: it should be an integral part of your overall business and strategic plan.

3   Ideally, you should include an exit plan in your business plan from start-up.

4   The exit planning components should include:
   *   establishing an exit date;
   *   choosing the optimum method of exit (and an alternative if the situation changes);
   *   setting targets for business growth and exit value;
   *   identifying the most likely potential purchasers (or type of purchasers) and what they are likely to want in a business;
   *   identifying and removing barriers to exit and impediments to sale.

5   How you are to achieve your targets should be outlined in the operational sections of your business plan.

6   You should bear in mind the timescale and chosen method of exit when you formulate your business development plans.

7   In the growth phase of your business you should review your plans and steer your business in the direction that your chosen exit option demands.

8   The type and extent of the business's development (or 'tailoring') should always be done with the chosen exit option in mind.

9   Where you wish to attract investors into the business, it is critical that you provide them with a comprehensive exit plan.

Figure 1.2. The exit planning process in summary.

A simple diagrammatic representation of the chronological steps of the exit planning process can be seen in Figure 1.3 below.

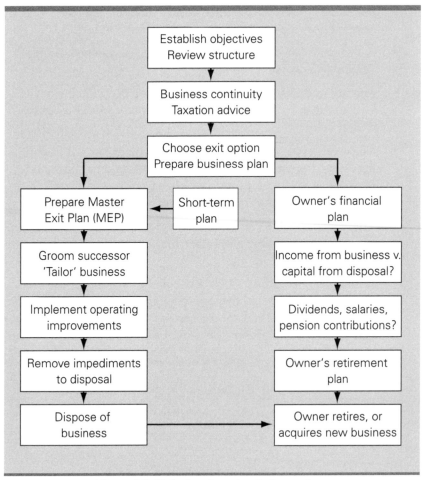

Figure 1.3. Exit planning: detailed overview.

SUMMARY

- It is important for business owners (and those going into business) to establish their business objectives.

- The primary business objectives of most small business owners are usually wealth creation and independence.

- These objectives will usually be achieved through a successful exit from a business.

- For family business owners, wealth creation objectives are coupled with the desire to pass on this wealth to heirs.

- A business can create wealth in two ways, namely income generation and capital creation.

- You are more likely to create wealth through owning a small business than by being employed, but only if you can create capital value in your business.

- The creation of the value is not enough on its own, it is also necessary for the business owner to undertake a successful disposal of business assets (which, in a family succession, includes a successful transfer to heirs).

- True independence can be achieved through owning a small business, but usually only after the successful exit of the owner.

- In summary, the primary business objectives of most business owners will only be achieved if they can successfully dispose of their businesses to a third party for value. This successful exit usually relies on effective exit planning.

2
Getting the right structure

In the previous chapter we looked at your business objectives as a first step in your exit planning. The next step is to review the ownership, management and operating structure of your business. This involves a review of how you should own your business (for example through a limited company, or a partnership), how the business is managed (for example, are you a one man band, or do you intend to have a management team?) and how you should approach other issues, such as accounting systems, service agreements and patents.

In this chapter I will examine how these issues influence your exit planning and why you might consider making changes to your structure to ensure the optimum return when you dispose of your business.

I will not address in detail the accounting, legal or taxation issues involved in how you should own or set up your business. For these you should seek advice from your advisers, bearing in mind your own circumstances. You could also refer to the start-up section in Helpful Reading, Appendix 4.

OWNERSHIP

You can own, or start-up, a business in many ways, for example as a sole trader, or through a partnership, or through a limited company, or by entering into a franchise agreement.

As a matter of interest, in the UK in 2003 54% of start-ups were sole traders, 24% were limited companies and 14% were partnerships. Businesses can change their structures as they develop, or to take advantages of changes in taxation laws, but no statistics are available for changes in structure after start-up.

Different business structures have both advantages and disadvantages with regard to such things as personal liability, taxation, compliance and accounting costs. There are commercial advantages in going into business with others (including combining capital resources and the complementary skills co-owners bring to the business), whilst there are also well-documented personal problems in having partners. I do not wish to address these pros and cons in any detail in this chapter; rather I will consider ownership from the perspective of exit planning.

To this end, I will consider the ownership options in three different circumstances, namely:

- Being in business on your own.
- Being in business with others.
- Owning a franchise.

BEING IN BUSINESS ON YOUR OWN

If you effectively own all of your business, you can operate either as a sole trader, or as a limited company. If your business is small and you run it on your own and you do not provide services where something can go wrong, there is no obvious reason to be anything other than a sole trader. The most important legal consideration of being a sole trader is that you are personably liable for all of your business and personal debts. If you are currently a sole trader and have any doubts about your circumstances, you should consult your accountant.

It is usual for a limited company to have more that one shareholder, but it is not necessary to have more than one. Complete management control of a company is secured by owning more than 75% of the shares. Some companies will have minority shareholders who own 1%, or less, of the company. In these circumstances, the 99% majority shareholder will, effectively, be a sole trader and have complete management control of the business, with the minority shareholders being nominal partners only.

From an exit planning point of view, it is easier to transfer part of a business to your family when it is a company (rather that a sole trader) by a simple gift of shares. This could be an important consideration for owners who are considering a family succession. Conversely, having minority shareholders of any size could lead to potential problems for the majority shareholder. (I will deal with minority shareholders and other exit planning issues involved in trading through a limited company later in this chapter.)

BEING IN BUSINESS WITH CO-OWNERS

If you are in business with other people (or intend going into business with others), you have a wider choice of how your business could be owned. The most common ownership structures for co-owners are a partnership or a limited company, although you could chose others such as a limited liability partnership (where each partner's liability is limited to the extent of their capital contributions and which can combine some of the benefits of a limited company with those of a partnership), or even a co-operative.

Partnerships

Partnerships are defined as relationships between persons who carry on business together for a profit and are governed by the Partnership Act 1890. For business owners, the main legal point to understand is that partners are responsible for each other's debts (other than debts relating to purely personal matters) and that each partner is also responsible individually (or, more precisely, 'jointly and severally') for all debts incurred by the partnership business, (which is also sometimes called a 'firm').

This responsibility for debts in a partnership contrasts with the 'limited liability' that business owners have in limited companies or limited liability partnerships. From this perspective alone, you could decide that a limited company or a limited liability partnership is a preferable structure through which to own your business. (You should note that a limited liability partnership is a relatively new business structure and few businesses in the UK have adopted this method of ownership.)

Should you decide to go into, or stay in a partnership, what are the implications for your exit planning? The first thing to consider is whether or not you have a partnership agreement and what the precise nature of its terms are.

a) Partnership agreements

Although partnerships are governed by the Partnership Act, the act does not adequately cover the ownership, financial and managerial relationships between partners. Consequently, it is wise for business partners to enter into a partnership agreement that more clearly deals with such things as the amount of their capital contributions, how profits are calculated and divided and what will happen if a partner wishes to exit.

Partnership agreements cover a wide range of issues and I will deal with them in more detail in Chapter 5. However, it might be worthwhile considering briefly some of the more important exit planning problems that arise when there is no partnership agreement in place.

If a partner leaves a partnership that has no partnership agreement, the partnership will dissolve and there will be no obligation for the remaining partners to pay the exiting partner for any business (or goodwill) value in his partnership share, other than any amounts owed to him from unpaid income or capital. Conversely, where a shareholder/director retires from a limited company he would still retain his shares, which could have a capital value, unless other shareholders have bought him out.

Where there is no partnership agreement, or an agreement exists that does not include a restraint of trade (or non-compete) clause, the exiting partner could be able to attract his old clients to his new business. He might then be able to sell this client base before retiring.

With no non-compete arrangements in place, should one of the partners leave the firm, take his clients with him and go into competition with the old partnership, the goodwill value of the firm and, therefore, the goodwill value of remaining partners' share of the firm could be worthless. Cashing in on this goodwill value could have been your exit strategy and your planned retirement fund!

Conversely, where you have a properly drawn-up partnership agreement, which includes an obligation (that is also adequately funded) on your partners, in certain circumstances, to buy you out for your share of the business value, this agreement could be a perfect exit strategy plan.

(Note: Many sole traders and partnerships have recently become limited companies – a process known as 'incorporating' – because of the favourable taxation treatment companies receive on their trading profits compared with sole traders and partnerships. This legislation was changed for the 2003/2004 tax year removing some of this apparent advantage. It is prudent in all cases to seek up-to-date professional advice, especially if you are thinking of changing your business structure.)

b) Capital Gains tax (CGT)

A vital aspect of exit planning is ensuring that you pay as little tax (including CGT) as is legally possible when you sell your business interests on exit. Current tax legislation provides relief (known as Business Asset Taper Relief) from the amount of CGT payable on gains made when disposing of 'qualifying' business assets.

For CGT purposes there is no difference between an individual owning business assets in a company or in partnership. I will deal with this in more detail in 'Limited companies' below, while a fuller explanation of the impact of taxation on exit planning is given in Chapter 10.

Limited companies

The basic legal concept of a company is that it is a separate legal entity from the shareholders who own it. A 'limited' company means that the obligations of the shareholders (also called members) are limited to the contribution they have made in purchasing their shares. In other words, shareholders of limited companies are not, in the normal course of events, liable for debts incurred by the company. The protection of limited liability is a reason many business owners incorporate their businesses.

However, this protection (also known as the 'corporate veil') can be illusory. For example, when a shareholder (who could also be a working director) is compelled by lenders to the company to provide a guarantee, this effectively renders the shareholder liable for the company's debts if the company fails to pay them. Also, the Companies Act imposes liability on directors for such things as the company's insolvent trading, which carries financial and other penalties.

But, what are the structural implications for exit planning in trading as a company? Firstly, we will consider the impact of taxation on your disposal proceeds.

a) The impact of taxation on the sale of shares

- **Capital Gains Tax (CGT)**

  You can own shares in a company in your own name, or through a holding company, or through a nominee company. There might be trading, or other, advantages in this sort of ownership, but from an exit planning point of view there are important taxation consequences to consider.

  1 Taper relief is available to certain kinds of companies only (called 'qualifying' companies) which are classified as 'trading' companies. Companies that undertake normal trading activities can be disqualified from being classified as trading companies for CGT purposes for such reasons as owning too many investment assets. If you own a company you should take advice to ensure you are classified by the Inland Revenue as a qualifying trading company.

  2 Taper relief from CGT applies to individuals, but not to companies. If you own the operating company's shares through a holding company, to qualify for taper relief this holding company must also be classified as a trading company. If its only subsidiary is the trading company in question, it too will be deemed a trading company, but if it has other subsidiaries that are not trading companies it will probably be deemed to be a non-trading company.

  3 Lastly, to get the full advantage of taper relief you must have owned your shares in the company for at least two years. This precludes last minute attempts to change ownership if you decide, or are forced to sell out. Note however, it *is* possible in some circumstances in transfers between spouses for the transferee to be deemed to have owned the shares for as long as the transferor.

- **Inheritance tax (IHT)**

  If you transfer property to a transferee (for example, shares to an heir) for less than market value (for example, as a gift) and die within seven years of the transfer, IHT will be payable by the transferee (in this case your heir).

  The theoretical impact and scope of IHT is the same whether the business is operating as a sole trader, partnership or limited company.

However, it is easier to pass on part of a business to heirs through gifting shares than it is to pass on part of a sole trader business. As with CGT, there are certain reliefs available under IHT legislation and if you plan to transfer business assets to your family you should obtain expert taxation advice. (IHT is covered in more detail in Chapter 10.)

b) Shareholders' agreements and minority shareholders

A shareholders' agreement is the company equivalent to the partnership agreement, which we have discussed above. It is just as important for shareholders to have agreements as it is for partners, particularly with regard to ensuring certainty in your exit planning. As a business owner you need complete flexibility on when and how to exit. If you have legal or technical barriers to exit, you lose this flexibility. Proper exit planning involves recognising these barriers and removing them. One such obvious barrier to exit is an uncooperative minority shareholder, an example of which I mentioned briefly in the last chapter.

With foresight, this problem can be avoided by entering into a shareholders' agreement that compels the minority shareholder to sell in certain defined circumstances. The best time to enter into a shareholders' agreement is either at business start-up or when shares are issued, as you can make it a condition of issuing the shares that an agreement is entered into. Once a problem has arisen the opportunity has passed.

Things look different, of course, from the perspective of minority shareholders, who have little power and influence in private companies. How do minority shareholders plan an exit when they can be out-voted on every issue and when they have no control of business strategy? The answer again lies in the shareholders' agreement, where minority shareholders, in some circumstances, can make their position more secure.

A detailed explanation of both shareholders and partnership agreements and the problems facing majority and minority shareholders is given in Chapter 5.

c) Different classes of shares

In the example of the problem with the recalcitrant minority shareholder mentioned in Chapter 1, we assumed, for simplicity, that the minority shareholder was the owner of the same class of share as the majority shareholder (i.e. that they were entitled to the same equity, voting and profit rights). One way for an entrepreneur to motivate, or reward business partners and colleagues in a business without giving them the same rights as himself, is to issue them with shares that have no voting or equity rights. This approach should ensure that minority shareholders are not a barrier to his exiting the business. (I discuss this in more detail in Chapter 4).

d) Purchasers and company accounts

A company's accounts, even where they are not audited, seem to have more credibility with (and are, perhaps, better understood by) prospective purchasers than the accounts of a sole trader, where personal and business entries could be intermingled. This might only be a matter of perception but could, nevertheless, still be important when negotiating a sale.

OWNING A FRANCHISE

There are several advantages in buying a franchise, but there are also various reasons why a franchise business is not for everyone. However, it is not the purpose of this book to examine these aspects of a franchise in any detail. Rather, I will concentrate on the important issues concerning franchising as a business structure as far as exit planning is concerned.

If you are thinking of buying a franchise you should seek expert professional advice. You could also go to Helpful Reading in Appendix 4 for guidance.

The importance of your franchise agreement

A franchise can be considered as a licence to operate a business using the franchisor's (or principal's) name, know-how and operating system. Your rights and obligations as a franchisee will be governed by the franchise agreement, which will establish, amongst other things:

- whether you own a business (as opposed to just having the right to operate one);
- the framework for deciding the value of your business;
- the ways you are able to dispose of it.

I cover these issues in some detail in Appendix 2 but, for convenience, I will summarise some of the more important issues here.

1) Do you own a business?

It is said that in Imperial Russia the distinction between possessing a business and owning one was perilously unclear as far as the mercantile class was concerned. Sometimes, this is true for franchisees in modern Britain. Although in most franchise agreements it is clear that the franchisee owns the business assets, from an exit planning standpoint the key question is whether the franchisee is able to sell the business to a third party for a capital sum during the period of the agreement, as opposed to losing all rights once the franchise agreement has expired.

However, in some franchise or licence arrangements, the question of ownership itself can still be unclear. An example of this is the financial services industry where the question arises of who 'owns' the clients and the goodwill value that arises from them.

In some industries, although the agent has no legal right either to the income from clients or any associated capital value resulting from this income once an agency agreement has terminated, the principal can, at its discretion agree that:

- income will continue to be paid to the agent after the agency agreement has terminated;
- benefits will continue to be paid to his beneficiaries after his death;
- agents can sell the benefits of the income to a third party (usually another agent) for a capital sum, subject to the purchaser being approved by the principal.

2) The value of a franchise business on exit

Assuming that you do own your franchise business, the next question that arises is does it have a value that you can realise on exit? The franchise agreement should cover the ways you are able to dispose of your business, how it is to be valued on sale and the conditions that need to be fulfilled by you, the franchisee, and the prospective purchaser before you can sell.

The market value of the franchisee business might also be influenced by the agreement, because it could dictate that the franchisee is selling in a market controlled by the franchisor, rather than in one that is free. This could depress the business's sale value. On the other hand, there could be positive factors in the agreement, such as if the franchisor offers to provide funding to purchasers, or itself offers to buy the business if the franchisee cannot dispose of it through normal channels.

3) Check your agreement

If you are a franchisee, the first exit planning step is to check what your agreement says about your principal's policy on exits. A well thought-out exit policy will not only include some restrictions on disposal, but should also include guidance and help for franchisees on the how to go about a sale or succession and, perhaps, provide for the granting of loans by the principal on favourable terms to purchasers.

MANAGEMENT STRUCTURE

It is well understood that a business's management structure is vitally important to its operating success. What is less well understood is how important management structure is when it comes to establishing a business's value on exit. In this section I will examine how management structure impacts on purchasers' perceptions of a business and the amount they are prepared to pay for it.

(Note: Ownership issues should be settled early [preferably from start up] but with management structure it is prudent to be flexible and to adapt your structure as your business grows and develops, always keeping in mind the nature and timing of your exit.)

'OWNER IS THE BUSINESS'

I first got involved with exit planning when I ran a mergers and acquisitions business in Australia. Many business owners would consult me about selling their businesses, although it was obvious that they were not fit to be sold, because of one or more impediments to sale (that is, reasons why the businesses would not fetch their asking prices). I would urge them to get advice on how they should best prepare their businesses for disposal and then return to me (after two or three years, if necessary) once the impediments had been removed and the business was ready for sale. When it became obvious that there were very few places that the business owners could obtain specialist exit planning advice, I decided to go into the exit planning advice business myself.

The real reason for this bit of background is to focus on the question of impediments to sale. Leaving aside that the most common impediment to sale I encountered was the over-inflated view owners had of the value of their businesses (a view not confined to *Australian* small business owners!), the next most common impediment was 'the owner was the business'. In other words, the owner ran, managed, drove and nurtured the business. He alone knew all the major clients and suppliers, understood how the factory was programmed and had all the management operating procedures in his head.

These businesses had no management. Certainly, they had employees, and often loyal and capable ones too, but none of them alone or together could run the business while the owner was away – a point emphasised by the fact that in most of them the owner had to telephone in every two days even when he was on holiday. The key question a hard-nosed purchaser would ask these owners in negotiations was: 'What have you got to sell?'

Consider for a moment the consequences of this sort of business from the perspective of the owner wishing to sell. Most owners wish to depart the business on, or shortly after, the sale. The purchaser, however, needs to be reassured that the business will continue to operate on, at least, the level of turnover and profit it had achieved prior to the purchase. Where the owner is the business there must be extreme risk that this will not happen unless he stays on as long as is necessary after sale to transfer his business 'know how' to the new owner. Unfortunately, even with an extended handover there are still risks involved. What happens, for example, if the owner should die just after sale? What happens if he is incapable of transferring his knowledge to the new owner? And, what happens if the old owner is unable (because, for example, of critical illness) to take part in an extended handover?

Whilst 'the owner is the business' does not necessarily always lead to the business not being sold, it will almost certainly restrict the market of potential buyers. These will be other owner managers with similar industry knowledge and technical background to the seller, or investors who have a suitably qualified management team they can put into the business. The other very important outcome will probably be a reduction in the price the owner was hoping to receive. Where the problem is real for purchasers they will insist on a price reduction to compensate for the difficulties they will have in running the business. Where it is not real, they will still use the apparent impediment as a bargaining weapon to negotiate down the price. Unfortunately, where the owner is the business he is on the back foot from the start of negotiations.

BUILDING A MANAGEMENT TEAM

The answer to the problem of the owner being the business is for the owner to work steadily towards replacing himself as the manager of the business, to make the business independent of him, so that when he goes on holiday the management do not even notice that he is away!

It is more likely that a business will grow and prosper in the long run if an owner 'works *on* and not *in*' the business, as the saying goes. However, what I am talking about here is the added value of a business on exit if an owner can make himself virtually redundant some time before he intends to sell, even if the short-term management costs are higher than is strictly necessary. (Note, when analysing 'real profits' of the business being sold, potential purchasers will take note that there has been some doubling up of management costs, which the purchaser will avoid if he is to manage the business himself.)

Where the owner has a layer of senior and/or middle management capable of running the business, the important point is to ensure that they remain in place when he comes to sell. Locking in key staff is a vital issue for all businesses and is brought into closer relief when the time of exit approaches. I will not examine here the general issue of how key staff can be locked into a business, as I address this issue in some detail in Chapter 4 on Business Continuity Planning. I do, however, later in this chapter look briefly at the potential difficulties that could arise with your exit planning when you use share options as a motivating and retention device.

(Note: Where owners employ key staff, the cost effectiveness of keyman insurance should be examined, regardless of the mechanisms you have in place to try to ensure management continuity, because having the cash resources to fill management gaps could be very useful.)

CREATING A MANAGEMENT STRUCTURE TO SUIT YOUR EXIT OPTION

This brings me to the wider issues of deciding on your method of exit and tailoring your management structure to fit this option. This is covered in detail in Chapter 9, but I wish to address some general issues here.

The management required to run a business will vary not only with the size of the business, but also with the type of business. This is relevant to exit planning because on disposal a business can:

- change from being one type of business to another. For example, from a private company to a public one;
- change in the type of management. For example, from a single owner-managed business to a business owned by its former management team, or from an owner-managed business with branch managers to a franchise organisation.

Different types of business require different types of management and exit planning requires that a business be positioned for this transition. For example, one of differences between a franchise business and a non-franchise business is that in a franchise the franchisor supplies a level of management expertise (on such things as buying, training and operating procedures) to the franchisee that a non-franchise business has to provide for itself. Also, the type of person suitable for branch management might not make a good franchisee.

Another example is where a company goes public. An issue that now arises is whether the company's management will be considered suitable to run a public company. This perceived suitability might not be restricted to pure operating management ability, but could include such things as personal standing and reputation in the business community.

As a final example, if your exit plan is to dispose of your business to your management (through a management buyout), the managers will probably need to satisfy their financial backers that they are not only adequate for their respective management tasks, but also that, as a team, they meet the financier's requirements of being suitably equipped for ownership.

WHEN TO GET THE MANAGEMENT STRUCTURE RIGHT

The owner of a business should not try to achieve the 'right' exit management structure from start-up. This is because, obviously, the management requirements of the business will change with the business's growth and it is unwise to burden it with unnecessary management costs in advance of requirements. The important point is to have the right management structure in place shortly before disposal, assuming the owner will leave when the business is sold.

THE BEST LAID PLANS...

Of course, it is not a perfect world and your plans could go awry. There are two areas that we have discussed above that could, in the event, go wrong. These are as follows:

1) Structuring your management to suit your buyers' needs

I have mentioned that purchasers will wish to acquire businesses that can be managed without the owner and that the best way to achieve this is to have a layer of competent management in place by the time of your sale. Unfortunately, although the first part of this statement will usually hold true (unless the owner's plan is to stay on indefinitely as an employee and this coincides with the purchaser's wishes), the second part might not.

Some purchasers desire to acquire businesses where they will put in their own management and, therefore, do not wish to acquire senior (or even middle) management employees. Having such management in place could, paradoxically, itself be an impediment for these particular purchasers.

A solution to this is to know your potential buyers and to tailor your business to suit. In practice, of course, it might be very difficult to know exactly who your purchaser will be, but you could anticipate the *type* of purchasers who could be interested. For example, will they be trade buyers from your industry (you might already have had informal talks about selling with some of them) or, perhaps, venture capitalists? What are their different requirements likely to be?

2) Using share options to lock in and motivate staff

Previously, I pointed out that share options are commonly used as a means of motivating and retaining key staff. In the UK share options are of two broad kinds, namely approved and unapproved. An example of an approved scheme is the Enterprise Management Incentive Scheme (EMIS), which was introduced by the Government in 2000. The scheme is available to companies with gross assets of not more than £30 million. Under the scheme the employee is granted the option to buy shares at a fixed price conditional on certain circumstances.

The company granting the options receives corporation tax relief for the cost of setting up and running the scheme, whilst there is no income tax or national insurance due on the grant of the option at market price. The employee will receive full taper relief from CGT on the sale of the shares within two years of the date of the grant.

Although there is no doubt that share schemes are widely used and are considered to be an effective way of locking in key staff (and should, therefore, be considered when retaining a management team is an important exit planning issue), I do not think that sufficient thought has been given to the downside of share option schemes when it comes to exit planning.

It is paramount that the business owner retains maximum exit planning flexibility, including the ability to sell 100% of the business when he so wishes. Where your company has granted an option to an employee that is still current, this option could still subsist when you sell your company. Consequently, any potential purchasers will know that they will have to inherit the option themselves and that this could result in their owning less than 100% of the company and, potentially, ending up with a stranger as a minority shareholder. The existence of a share option scheme could, therefore, make the business less attractive and could be what I call 'a barrier to exit', that is, something that makes a business more difficult to sell, or less valuable in the eyes of potential purchasers.

So, although the share option might have seemed to you originally to be an effective way of retaining a key manager to facilitate your exit, it could turn out to be an unwanted headache when it comes to satisfying a potential purchaser who is only interested in 100% of your business. Of course, like most other business problems, a solution is possible at a price and you could always buy out the option. However, this costly solution can be avoided with forward planning. In Chapter 5 on shareholders' agreements I will explain a way in which the potential problem can be avoided.

ATTRACTING INVESTORS

Your exit from a business can be accomplished in stages. It might be part of a company strategy to sell shares to investors as stage one and later, as stage two, to sell all the shares in a secondary buy-out, or to list the company on the Stock Exchange. If your potential investors are professional venture capitalists they will be very careful about investing their money and you will need to ensure all aspects of your business are structurally sound before you seek this investment. Examples of areas that might need attention to attract investors include intellectual property, directors' service contracts, legal contracts and accounting systems.

INTELLECTUAL PROPERTY

You need to decide whether your intellectual property can be patented and, if so, you should consider doing this immediately. But proceed with caution. Securing a patent is expensive, so it is not worth proceeding unless there is a clear commercial benefit either in earning income or protecting your business from disruption. Also, to attract investors it is important that the intellectual property rights are clearly owned by the company and not, for example, by the directors. (The securing of patents is a complicated matter and expert advice should be obtained before you decide to proceed.)

DIRECTORS' SERVICE CONTRACTS

In Chapter 5, I discuss the importance of companies with co-owners having shareholders' agreements (that usually include directors as parties to the agreement). Professional investors will insist on such agreements to cover their position as shareholders should they invest. However, whether you currently have a shareholders' agreement in place or not, it will be important in a company seeking investors to have service contracts for directors that include details of remuneration and notice periods, restraint of trade (non-compete) clauses and delineation of directors' powers.

LEGAL CONTRACTS

In Chapter 8, I explain that not having contracts in place with suppliers, or customers, (or principals where you act as agent), is an impediment to sale. These contracts are best entered into as soon as the relationship is established and not just before exit. In my experience, existing contracts are often allowed to lapse causing some panic when due diligence by the purchaser reveals this fact. The key point, therefore, is not only to enter into these formal arrangements, but also to ensure they remain current.

ACCOUNTING SYSTEM

It is necessary for many reasons that you install and maintain an accounting system that is simple and accurate and complies with accounting standards. Not the least important reason for this is that it enables you to manage your business properly. In the exit-planning contest it is important because, firstly, buyers (especially private ones) do not like to be confronted by unnecessarily complicated accounts and, secondly, the standard of your accounting system reflects on the quality of the business in the eyes of investors and purchasers. Indeed, purchasers might even judge your business by the quality of its professional and business advisers.

SUMMARY

In this chapter we have looked at the importance of ownership, management and legal structure in exit planning. In summary, we have seen that:

- There are various legal ways that a business can be owned, including as a sole trader, partnership, limited company or as a franchisee, and each of them has an influence on how you should plan an exit.

- Ownership structure should be addressed as soon as possible, preferably from start-up.

- Where you are in business with others, partnership and shareholders' agreements are key elements in exit planning.

- The type of company you own, how you own it and how long you have owned the shares are crucial taxation issues in exit planning.

- Minority shareholders might not present operating or managerial problems to majority owners, but they can provide obstacles to a smooth exit.

- If you are a franchisee you could have particular problems when planning an exit and it is vital that franchisees are aware of any exit restrictions contained in their franchise agreements.

- There are serious problems in selling a business when 'the owner is the business' and in these, and most other, circumstances it is crucial to have a management team in place before you exit.

- Different types of businesses might need individual managers with the personal attributes that are appropriate to the type of business, whilst different types of businesses definitely need different management structures.

- It is important to plan your management structure with your optimum exit option in mind and, where possible, with your particular purchaser in mind.

- It is vital that you to retain key staff, particularly as you approach exit and during the exit process itself.

- Management structure needs to be addressed as the business develops through its growth stages and should be 'right' by the time of exit.

- Sometimes, the best-laid plans go awry, particularly with establishing what you believe to be the 'right' management structure and retaining key managers through share options.

- Issues such as protecting intellectual property, entering and maintaining contracts with suppliers and principals and having service contracts with directors all need attention when a business is trying to attract investors or purchasers.

3

When, why and how will you exit?

In this chapter we will consider the reasons business owners give for wanting to exit and why, in the event, they actually do exit. We look at the interrelationship between the reasons for exit, when to exit, the amount of time available for exit and the exit options that could be available in this time frame. All these factors could influence the effectiveness of exit planning and, consequently, the amount the owner will receive for his business on disposal.

We next consider how your exit success can be influenced by other considerations. For example, were you able to exit through the method you chose, or did something unforeseen prevent this? Or, were economic conditions favourable for exit at the time you chose? What will insolvency do to your exit plans?

We then consider what can be achieved by the business owner should you embark on either a short-, medium- or long-term exit plan. And, finally we help you to decide whether embarking on a long-term plan is worth your while.

INTRODUCTION

Don Panoz, the 69-year old founder of St Andrews Bay Resort, who was fit and active, when asked why he was selling half his business, replied: 'The clock doesn't lie.'

Most business owners would like to exit their businesses in their own time and in the manner of their choosing. But, unfortunately, there are many external and interlocking factors at play that can determine when exit decisions are made and how an exit might come about. For example:

- the **reason for exit** will probably establish **when you exit** (for example, retirement when you reach 60 in 10 years);
- when you exit will influence **the amount of time** you have to plan;
- which, in turn, could establish **the method of exit** (due to the amount of time available and necessary to prepare properly for the exit method you have chosen).

EXPECTED REASONS FOR EXITING

When examining the reasons for exiting a business, we must distinguish between what business owners think will cause them to exit their businesses from the reasons why an exit actually happens.

When asked what will cause them to exit, the usual reason given by business owners is reaching 'normal' retirement age (which for most owners is about 60). This reason supplies both a *why* and a *when* answer, as the owner has a specific retirement age in mind. Owners also give the following reasons for exiting:

- Receiving a good offer for the business.
- Getting fed up/tired/bored/disillusioned with the business.
- When the business is worth a specific target value.
- If the business does not reach specific profit targets.
- If the business does not provide a reasonable living within a specified period.
- When a son/daughter/etc. is ready to take over and manage the business.
- When management or employees are ready to purchase the business.

You will notice that most of these reasons (other than, perhaps, where a target value is being aimed at) are open-ended as to time and do not, necessarily, set a target exit date, or establish an exit time frame.

ACTUAL EXIT REASONS

It is interesting to note that there are many other reasons (besides the anticipated reasons given above) why owners actually decide to exit their businesses. These include personal and business reasons.

a) The owner's personal reasons could be:

- a fall out with partners or shareholders (including family shareholders);
- family reasons, such as a divorce;
- ill health, necessitating an early retirement;
- to take up an employment opportunity;
- pure desire for change.

b) Business reasons could be:

- the business goes broke/is insolvent;
- it fails to reach minimum levels of income or profit.

The points to note here are the following:

- most of these reasons are unexpected or, at least, are not the reasons why a business owner would wish to exit;
- those owners who exit for the reasons they expect are able to plan within a time frame of their making;
- most business owners are compelled to exit for unanticipated reasons and, consequently, within a much shorter time frame than they had hoped. This will, probably, influence both the method and effectiveness of their exit.

TIME AVAILABLE AND THE METHOD OF EXIT

As you have seen, the reason for your exit (whether planned or otherwise) could have a direct influence on when the exit will take place. When the exit takes place will, obviously, influence the time you have to plan and, perhaps the method of exit employed. These factors could have a profound impact on the effectiveness of your planning and, consequently, the amount you receive for your business on disposal. Let us look at what

I mean by this.

Assume that you plan to leave your business to your son. Having read this book, you are aware that grooming an heir for succession is a time-consuming task if it is to be done effectively. Consequently, you set up a 10-year plan to undertake the various steps necessary to prepare your son for the eventual role of running the business. Unfortunately, within a year you fall seriously ill. You have no time to continue with the grooming of your son and he is unprepared to take over the business. Also, there is no time available to investigate and arrange other possible exit routes, such as a management buy-out or a public flotation.

Most exit options are now closed to you and you will, probably only have the option of selling through a trade sale, if you are sufficiently well to arrange it. If you are unable to organise a trade sale, the business might be forced to sell its assets at fire sale prices and close down.

Your original plan to exit through a family succession would probably have had two main objectives, namely:

1 Financial objectives You planned to sell the business to your son for an agreed price and, perhaps, accepted that payment would be made over time. Because you controlled the transaction, the price and payment terms could be tailored to fit your retirement plans.

2 Personal objectives You wanted your son to take over the business, continue the family connection and be a business success. You would continue to work in the business in a consulting capacity until you decided to retire completely.

Unfortunately, because you have fallen ill and have been forced to abandon your succession plan and sell the business through a trade sale, neither your financial nor personal objectives have been achieved.

THE LESSONS TO BE LEARNT

What lessons can we learn from this? Should all planning be abandoned because of the uncertainties of business and life? Not at all. I recommend that in planning for your exit you should take the following approach:

1   Determine why you wish to exit.

2 Consider whether this reason establishes (more or less) your exit date, or whether you need to set one.

3 Using this exit date as your target, assess the time available to you to plan your exit and choose the most favourable method of exit for your business. (You will learn more about this when you read Chapters 6 and 7.)

4 Proceed planning on this basis, but recognise that your plans could be derailed by unforeseen events (and that you might need a Plan B).

5 Most importantly of all: **begin your planning immediately, because you never know how much time you will have to execute your plan.**

THE EFFECTIVENESS OF YOUR EXIT

The exit method you choose and the amount of time you allow yourself to implement your exit plan will influence the effectiveness of your planning and your ability to achieve your exit goals. Failure to meet these goals can usually be attributed to one of five main reasons, namely:

1 You have not allowed yourself sufficient time to implement your exit plan through the particular exit option you had chosen.

2 Your actual method of exit is not the one you had planned.

3 You are prevented from implementing your plan fully because of unforeseen circumstances.

4 The economic circumstances in your industry (or in the economy as a whole) are unfavourable for business sales at the time you were forced to sell.

5 Your business becomes insolvent.

We will now consider these reasons in more detail.

1) INSUFFICIENT TIME TO IMPLEMENT YOUR EXIT PLAN

It is advantageous if business owners choose an exit option that will result in the maximum financial return for them on disposal. (I call this the optimum exit option). However, it is also necessary that you allow sufficient time to implement the exit plan that the particular exit option demands.

For example: You resolve that you need to retire in four years for health reasons. You decide that the optimum exit option is to list your company on the Alternative Investment Market in London (AIM) when its annual profits have reached the minimum level needed for it to receive institutional support.

You calculate that it will take you at least four years for profits to reach this figure. You proceed with your plans on this basis.

However, after three years it becomes obvious that the business will not meet its minimum profit targets, but you still wish to retire within 12 months. Your business is now unable to list on the AIM and will be forced into some other exit method.

2) THE METHOD OF EXIT WAS NOT THE ONE YOU HAD PLANNED

Using the example above, if you are unable to list on the AIM you will need to resort to another exit method, or postpone your exit date. In this case, as your health is worsening, you cannot postpone your exit, so you will have to attempt the exit through another method, say a trade sale. You could have two major problems now, namely:

- the sale will be conducted under pressure and potential purchasers will probably utilise this fact to your disadvantage;
- the business was being 'tailored' and prepared for listing, which will not necessarily mean that it is suitable for a trade buyer. (Please refer to Chapter 9 for more information on 'tailoring'.)

The likely outcome is that although the business is disposed of via a trade sale, the price is substantially less than the valuation that would have been put on the business through a listing. Another possible outcome is that the business could be broken up and its assets sold at fire sale prices.

3) The intervention of unforeseen circumstances

Again using the above example, let us assume slightly different circumstances. You begin with your plans to list on the AIM, but after two years fall seriously ill. You have followed the chosen method of exit, but your business is not ready to list.

Unfortunately, you now find yourself in the same circumstances as are described in (2) above.

4) Unfavourable economic circumstances at time of sale

Where circumstances force you to exit in a hurry (perhaps because of ill health) it is possible that the time of your exit could coincide with a slump in the general economy, or in your particular industry, thus further adversely affecting your selling price. This adverse effect will apply whatever your exit option except, perhaps, a family succession.

Should you have to sell because of the death of a partner or shareholder (particularly where there is no shareholders' agreement in place) you might have to act immediately with no time at all to plan. Here you will have to sell the business in whatever way you can and whatever the economic climate.

When there is no pressure on you to dispose of your business you can adjust your target exit date to coincide with favourable economic conditions.

5) The effect of insolvency

If the directors of a company believe a company is insolvent they have an obligation to either re-capitalise the company, or to enter into a voluntary arrangement with creditors, or to cease to incur further credit (which effectively means ceasing to trade), or to wind it up. All these outcomes, other than the re-capitalisation will, obviously, have a dramatic impact on any plan to exit the business through conventional methods.

As insolvency is a complex subject, I will spend a moment to explain some of its potential consequences.

Where a sole trader decides that his business is insolvent, there is no legal obligation on him to cease trading, although one would expect that, for his own economic well-being and peace of mind, he would take every step possible to reduce his deficit through returning to profitability, or to cease trading.

With companies there are several issues, some of which overlap, to be taken into account by directors in deciding whether their company is insolvent, but unfortunately there is no legal definition of insolvency.

One issue to consider is whether a company is able to pay its debts as and when they fall due, or is able to reach agreement on their payment, or to provide acceptable security for them. Another consideration is whether the value of a company's liabilities exceeds the value of its assets. On a pure net asset test a company might be technically insolvent, but it can continue to trade quite legally if it has the finance available to pay its current debts, or has made suitable arrangements with its creditors for payment, and has good reason to believe that its prospects will improve.

The converse is also true: some businesses could appear to have strong net assets (perhaps because of overvaluation of such things as intangibles or inter-company receivables) but still fall into cash flow difficulties and, as a result, could be wound up. The sad fact that many business owners discover is that assets are not cash, and without cash (or access to finance) you cannot continue to trade.

The decision that directors need to make regarding solvency is important for at least two reasons. Firstly, the onus is on directors to make a determination on solvency on a continuing basis so as to avoid any possible legal action for wrongful trading. Secondly, the way in which a company is wound up is dependent, among other things, on whether or not it is solvent.

Where a business owner is considering closing down a business, insolvency will affect the exit choices available to him. The best way to close down a business from the owner's point of view is to go through a process of a solvent managed close down with a managed sell off of assets at market prices. The worst way is, probably, a liquidation with sale of assets at fire sale prices and the added burden of the liquidator's costs.

Figure 3.1, below shows the interrelation between the various factors we have discussed so far. It shows how and when you wish to exit (or are forced to exit) influences when you might exit which, in turn, influences or limits, what method (or option) you might adopt to exit.

It then considers how the method of exit will be determined by whether your company is solvent or insolvent. Becoming insolvent means you have limited opportunities to plan an exit and will, probably, lead to an immediate disposal of the business and/or its assets. If your business is solvent, obviously you should have time to plan for an exit through conventional methods.

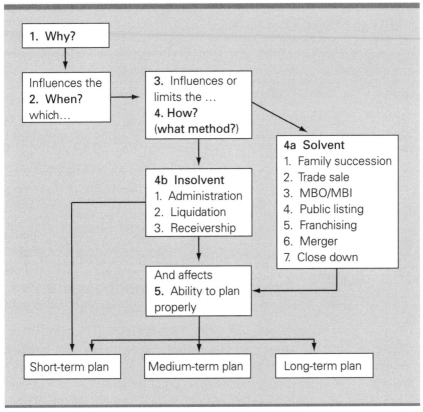

Figure 3.1. Why, when and how.

As you can see from Figure 3.1, the next issue to consider is what can be accomplished in short-, medium- or long-term exit planning.

SHORT-, MEDIUM- AND LONG-TERM PLANNING

We have seen above how time constraints (brought about by lack of planning or chance) can reduce the effectiveness of your planning. It might be useful to consider in more detail what can be done when you are able to plan over various periods of time, which I will call short-, medium- and long-term planning. I consider a short-term plan to be anything under two years, a medium-term plan to be between two and four years and a long-term plan to be for more than four years.

To help you make a decision on what time frame is necessary for implementing your exit plan, we list in Figure 3.2, below the typical steps involved in successful exit planning.

Typically, an exit plan will involve you taking all, or some, of the following steps:

1 Deciding your exit time frame.
2 Getting your structure right, including legal structure, taxation issues and shareholders' agreements.
3 Choosing your optimum exit option.
4 Tailoring your business to suit your exit option.
5 Grooming of management or successor.
6 Removing impediments to sale.
7 Growing business value through acquisitions and/or organic growth.
8 Finalising disposal preparations, for example preparing a memorandum of offer, advertising for sale, etc., and, perhaps some of the more cosmetic cleaning up of the business's appearance.
9 Integrating your personal financial (or retirement planning) with your exit planning.
10 Disposing of the business.

These steps will be clearer once you have read this book.

Figure 3.2. The exit planning steps.

We will now consider how effectively each of these steps can be taken under each planning time frame.

THE SHORT-TERM PLAN

Any short-term exit plan is a compromise. If you are unable or unwilling to delay your disposal for at least two years, you will be severely limited in what you can do to improve the value and saleability of your business.

The shorter your planning period the harder it will be to prepare your business properly for exit. Using the 10 steps in Figure 3.2 as a guideline, we summarise below what you are able to achieve in this time frame as follows:

Step 1: Time frame

You have chosen a short-term plan (or one has been forced on you).

Step 2: Structure

a) Although you will have time to enter into a shareholders' agreement, you might find it difficult at this late stage to get your fellow shareholders to agree with your terms, particularly if they know you want to exit shortly.

b) Tax minimisation: Under current tax laws you are required to own assets in your own name for a minimum of two years to take full advantage of business asset taper relief from Capital Gains Tax.

Step 3: Choosing the optimum exit option

You are limited in your choice of exit option, because of the amount of time that is needed to prepare for some options (see above).

Step 4: Tailoring your business to suit your exit option

This is something that should, ideally have begun at start-up. This is not something that can be done with only two years to exit.

Step 5: Grooming of management or successor

It is not easy to generalise here, but you would usually need two to four years to groom senior management to take over ownership of your business, while some family succession experts advise allowing 15 years to groom successfully an heir for owner/management. The actual time required will depend on the quality of the management and the personal attributes of the successor, but a period of two years' grooming for managers and five for heirs is probably the minimum.

Step 6: Removing impediments to sale

As you would expect, some impediments take more time to remove than others. For example, should your major impediment be that your business has only two or three customers and you are advised that to be attractive to buyers it should have at least 20, you could find that this will take several years to accomplish. Conversely, if your impediments are largely cosmetic (such as your business looking run down and untidy) these can be rectified within two years. (You can learn more about impediments to sale in Chapter 8.)

Step 7: Growing the business

Growth through acquisitions is possible, but unlikely, in the time frame allowed. You will usually achieve only limited organic growth in two years.

Step 8: Disposal preparations

These, by their nature, are short-term activities that you will be able to accomplish in a short-term plan.

Step 9: Integration of personal and business planning

Personal financial planning is a long-term enterprise and little of note could be accomplished in this regard over the short term.

Step 10: Disposal

The length of your planning is not a major factor here.

THE MEDIUM-TERM PLAN

With two to four years to implement your exit plan you should be successful in achieving most of your exit objectives, depending on the size of the business and, of course, on the extent of its problems. Using Figure 3.2, above, as a guide and bearing in mind what you can achieve in the short term you can, obviously, also achieve in the medium term, I comment only on major differences between short- and medium-term planning as follows:

Step 3: You have more room here to choose from the full range of exit options, although time will be tight for a public listing, setting up a franchisor business and transferring your business through a family succession (specifically in respect to grooming an heir).

Step 4: If your exit is in four years, you should be able to tailor your business for the chosen exit option.

Step 5: Two to four years should be sufficient time to groom a management team but not, necessarily, to train a successor for owner/management.

Step 6: As stated previously, the successful removal of your impediments to sale will depend on what they are, but the more time you allow yourself to implement your exit plan the more successful you should be in removing impediments.

Step 7: You should be able to make progress in increasing the business's turnover and profitability, although many owners underestimate the time it takes to turn around, or grow a business.

Step 8: This should not present you with any problems.

Step 9: Although you have more time to address your financial planning, it will still not be sufficient if you have not begun your planning years earlier.

THE LONG-TERM PLAN

A planning period of over four years is probably the minimum for you to achieve most of your exit strategy aims. However, time alone will not necessarily mean that you will achieve all your growth and value targets and, similarly, having a longer time to remove impediments to sale does not guarantee that they will be removed.

IS IT WORTH IMPLEMENTING A LONG-TERM PLAN?

Where you are keen to exit as soon as possible, but have the opportunity of delaying the implementation of a long-term exit plan, you might wish to be sure that such a plan has sufficient advantages compared with a shorter-term plan. Figure 3.3 below, should help clarify this issue for you.

Checklist

1 Check the current market conditions for business disposals in general, and for your type of business in particular. A corporate broker, or an accountant, or a specialist corporate adviser could be good sources of advice.

  • What you wish to know is whether there is currently a strong demand for your type of business and whether prices are good.

  • Try to get consensus on the current trend of the economy. (For example, are things likely to be better or worse over the next three years?)

2 Check with your accountant your likely tax position and whether delaying your sale has advantages for you.

3 Review your business's operations.

  • Are there any obvious things that currently depress its sale value, or make it more difficult to sell?

  • Can these be rectified, and how long do you think it will take? (You should refer to Chapter 8 'Impediments to Sale' for guidance here.)

4 Check whether your fellow shareholders wish to sell and the position with your shareholders'/partners'agreements.

  • For example, at what price will minority shareholders sell?

  • Are they compelled to sell when you sell?

  • What prices are you compelled to pay them if you are forced to buy them out first?

  • Is a delay prudent, or even essential to sort this out?

5 Check whether your management will stay on after the sale. For example, is there anything in your management agreements that covers this?

Figure 3.3. Is it worth implementing a long-term plan?

You should review your position having considered the issues in Figure 3.3. This will give you a good idea of the problems you are likely to have with a short-term sale and the upside that is possible through delaying an immediate sale and implementing a longer-term plan.

CREATING THE IDEAL BUSINESS

In all exit planning, whatever the time frame, the aim should be to create a business that is highly attractive to potential buyers, what you might call the ideal business. Although you will probably fall short, this could still be your aim. Generally speaking, you will get closer to your aim the longer you have to implement your plans.

It could be helpful if you remember three important exit planning rules, namely:

- start your planning now;
- have a sense of urgency;
- be thorough in implementing your plans.

SUMMARY

In this chapter we have considered a variety of issues that arise from how much time you have to implement your exit plans. These can be summarised as follows:

- Because of the inherent uncertainties of life you never know how much time you might have to plan your exit.

- It is sensible, therefore, to begin your exit planning as soon as you can.

- The amount of time you give yourself to plan can determine the exit options available to you.

- The longer you have to plan the more likely it is that you will achieve your objectives.

- Insolvency will severely limit your exit choices and the likelihood of achieving a reasonable return from disposal of your business assets.

- By going through a series of questions you can establish whether it is worth your while to engage in a long-term exit plan rather than selling immediately.

4

Business Continuity Planning

In this chapter we will look at the personal, family and other risks involved in owning a business and how managing these will give you a better chance to achieve a successful exit. This management of these risks is sometimes known as Business Continuity Planning.

First we consider what steps you can take to minimise personal and family risks in your business. We do this by going through a worksheet that asks you various questions to highlight your circumstances and possible risks, which then leads to suggested solutions.

A key aspect of Business Continuity Planning is having agreements between partners and shareholders (co-owners), so next we consider some of the pros and cons of having co-owners in your business. We recognise that having co-owners does have some obvious advantages, but point out that it also has large potential risks, not least because co-owners can hamper your exit. (In the next chapter we see how shareholders' or partnership agreements can minimise the exit risks posed by co-owners, but in this chapter we help you decide whether you should consider having co-owners at all.)

Next, we consider how issuing different classes of shares to potential co-owners can limit their power to influence your exit decisions. This leads us to look at the status of minority shareholders in a private company and how this affects their ability to exit.

Continuing with the worksheet we now consider the necessity of having a will and what steps you can take to protect a business from the potential divorce of the business owner, or of one of his heirs, by for example, the use of a trust.

Finally, we confirm the usefulness of insurance in guarding against the loss of key staff and the necessity of obtaining expert taxation advice before you make final decisions.

INTRODUCTION

Business Continuity Planning is the term used for the management of the risks in a business associated with events that might happen to co-owners, key employees and you and your family. The events include such things as death, serious illness, disputes and divorce. The management of them includes such things as the entering into of shareholders' agreements, undertaking financial planning, writing wills, setting up trusts, insurance and taxation planning.

Management of people risk is a very large subject and in this chapter I concentrate only on issues that impinge directly on exit planning, namely co-owners and personal and family risk; whilst in the next chapter I cover shareholders' agreements.

But, first I would like you to consider the wider question: 'Do I need a Business Continuity Plan?' The worksheet Figure 4.1, below takes you through a series of questions to clarify what aspects of a business continuity plan you should be considering in your particular circumstances.

You can go through the worksheet as follows:

- Starting from the top, the figure asks you to consider whether you have partners or fellow shareholders. If the answer is yes, a shareholders' agreement is required. We return to this later on.
- If the answer is no, obviously you do not require a shareholders' agreement and we move to the right of the worksheet.
- You now need to consider if you have heirs. If the answer to this is also no, you still need to consider what will happen to your business assets when you die.
- Where you have no partners or fellow shareholders, but do have an heir, you need to consider whether you require a will to ensure your

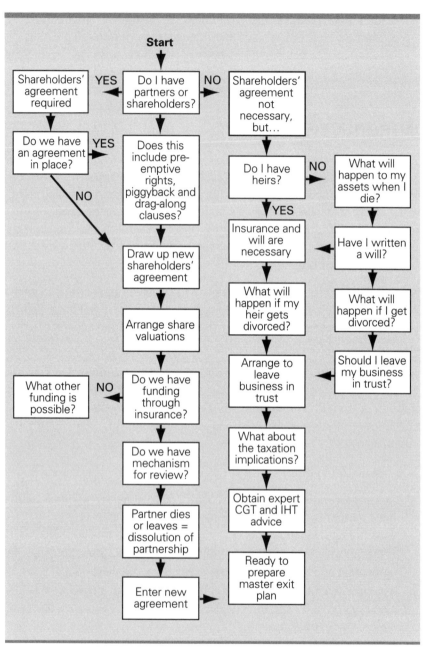

Figure 4.1. Do I need a Business Continuity Plan?

wishes are fulfilled – if you are married, for example, and wish to leave your business to your offspring and not your spouse, you will need a will to ensure this happens.

- Next you will need to consider the implications of your heir becoming divorced before he has inherited the business and whether it would be wise to put the business into a discretionary trust with the heir as a named beneficiary.

- Finally, under this option, you need to consider the taxation implications (especially Inheritance Tax) of all this and obtain expert advice, if necessary.

- Returning now to the top or the figure, if you do have fellow shareholders or partners you require a shareholders' (or partnership) agreement. If you already have one in place, you need to check that it adequately covers the matters addressed in the next chapter, especially the circumstances surrounding the sale of shares and interests.

- If it does, does it also address the valuation of these interests, the funding mechanism that will facilitate the purchase, and a provision for regular review of value, and that the funding is still adequate?

- Finally, with a partnership agreement does it remove the problem that a partner's leaving usually gives rise to the necessity of a new agreement?

- Having covered the risks associated with your particular circumstances (including drawing up a shareholders' agreement, writing a will, taking out insurance, putting your business into trust and obtaining expert tax advice), the figure confirms that you are now in a position to prepare your Master Exit Plan.

Now that we have established the parameters of your Business Continuity Planning, we will turn to the central question of whether or not you should consider having co-owners in your business.

HAVING CO-OWNERS IN YOUR BUSINESS

Co-owners in a business are either shareholders (who own shares in a company), or partners (who own interests in the capital of a partnership). Co-owners should be distinguished from directors and employees, who may or may not be shareholders, no matter how senior or important they may be. Co-owners can be passive shareholders, such as sometimes happens with venture capitalists; or active ones, such as working shareholders who are also directors or employees.

The decision to have partners or fellow shareholders in your business is a difficult one, which could have a profound effect on your ability both to plan for, and to execute a successful exit. The information in this chapter should assist you in making this decision.

Where two or more entrepreneurs have decided that by pooling their combined financial resources and skills base they could start a successful business together, the issue is not so much whether to have co-owners, but how best to regulate their relationships. How this should be done is explained in the next chapter on shareholders' and partnership agreements.

So, what are the issues to consider when a business owner (or someone thinking of starting a business) thinks he would like to, or needs to bring in a co-owner?

THE REASONS FOR WANTING CO-OWNERS

Where you are considering having a co-owner, you have an opportunity before committing to this path of evaluating the pros and cons of this proposition. In this regard, it might assist you to consider why others have thought if necessary to work with co-owners.

When I have asked business owners why they thought they needed to bring in a co-owner, the most common reasons given have been as follows:

- the potential co-owners will provide the additional (or start-up) capital that the business needs;
- the need to add technical and/or managerial support to the business, which is best achieved by offering equity to the individuals with these skills;
- the desire to lock in, reward or motivate existing key staff members by providing shares or share options;

- the need to placate family members by bringing them into the business.

Your own reasons for wishing to have a co-owner could be included in this list. But, is bringing in a co-owner the only or, indeed, the best solution to the problem? Are there alternative ways to achieve your objectives?

ARE THERE ALTERNATIVES TO HAVING CO-OWNERS?

Before we consider the alternatives to having co-owners, I wish to make the general point that there are always potential risks in having co-owners in a business and that you should be sure that the advantages of having them outweigh the disadvantages. Two of the most obvious risks with having co-owners are as follows:

- The risk of fall out between you and your co-owner and the subsequent risk to your business and possible major disruption to your life. (Think of how many unfortunate examples you personally know where this has happened!)
- The risk that your co-owner will make it difficult for you to exit the business at the time and at the price of your choosing.

Bearing these in mind, we can now look at the most common reasons given for taking in co-owners and analyse whether there are other ways of achieving the same results.

THE NEED FOR ADDITIONAL CAPITAL

For an established business there are usually two reasons why additional capital is required. The first is for business growth or expansion (either through acquisition or organic growth) and the second is to fund trading losses. The questions you need to ask yourself are whether you really need the extra money and whether you can raise this funding from external sources in the form of debt, without the need to sell equity in your business.

a) In the case of requiring capital for expansion, the first step you could take is to ensure that you have produced a realistic business plan with rigorously tested cash flow forecasts that show unequivocally that you need the extra funding. If this is indeed the case, the next step is to consider why you are considering bringing in an equity partner. Is it because you cannot raise the money elsewhere, or is it because the prospective partner also brings other assets to the business, such as a technical or professional skill that you do not possess and which is not easy to acquire elsewhere? On the question of raising the money elsewhere, have you approached the likely funders, such as a high street bank; or have you avoided this because you do not have a professionally produced business plan?

b)   In many under-performing businesses the idea that additional capital will solve the problem is a misconception. Often, throwing money at the business is not a solution to the problem, it merely delays discovery of the solution. If your business is losing money, the first thing you need to establish is does the business really need extra capital, or does the answer to its problems lie elsewhere, perhaps in closer cost control, or expansion of the product line, or reducing your own drawings?

If, after thorough analysis of your capital requirements, you still believe your business needs extra funding, be it for expansion, capital equipment, or working capital, you now need to consider the following:

a)   Is the capital a long-term requirement, or a short-term one?

b)   Do you personally have the resources (assets or security) to provide this extra capital?

c)   Can the capital be secured from sources of loan funds, including:
   •   traditional lenders, such as banks?
   •   family or friends?
   •   government agencies?

If you decide, in the event, that the only way you are going to secure the funds you need is through issuing shares to others, you could still do it in a way that could maintain your complete control over the company and your exit planning flexibility. For example, you could issue shares of a different class to your own shares. These could be shares that are entitled to a preferential dividend and repayment at their face value (or value at which they were issued), but have no voting rights, or rights to a share of capital proceeds in a winding up or sale. By issuing such shares you achieve your objective of raising extra capital, without having a shareholder who could compromise your ability to sell 100% of the company.

THE NEED TO ACQUIRE TECHNICAL AND/OR MANAGEMENT SKILLS

Here you could consider whether you are able to achieve your goals by employing additional senior management in your business without having to make them equity partners. Also, can you get access to the skills you require by using outside contractors on a user-pays basis?

LOCKING IN AND REWARDING STAFF BY PROVIDING SHARES OR SHARE OPTIONS

There are many ways of locking in and rewarding staff other than by issuing shares or share options. The most common form of incentive has traditionally been the bonus.

Bonuses can be for individuals or for teams. They are excellent where performance can be easily measured, such as achieving sales (for individuals) or profit targets (for all employees). The key to a successful bonus scheme is fairness and simplicity, although when applied to the whole staff you might need to consider weighting reward to levels of salary, service and attendance record. Rewards can be in the form of cash or other benefits in kind, such as travel, increased holidays or health insurance.

If you feel however, that you need to issue shares (or share options) to lock in key staff members, you could consider issuing a different class of share from your own. A company is free to issue almost any kind of share it chooses. These can be shares with preferential entitlement to dividends with voting powers, the same entitlement to dividends as the ordinary shareholders but with no voting rights attached, no entitlement to dividends, or any combination thereof.

The point of this from an exit-planning viewpoint is that you can motivate and lock in staff by giving them a stake in the company without their becoming an encumbrance on your unfettered right to exit your business and transfer 100% of the equity.

From the owner's point of view you need to consider whether your prime motivation is to achieve business goals, or to lock in key employees on whom your business relies. If you are looking to lock in key employees, it is important to find out what motivates them before selecting the incentives offered, but always bearing in mind that co-owners can be a bit of a nuisance!

THE NEED TO PLACATE FAMILY MEMBERS

This is an area in which there is some disagreement amongst family business owners and specialist advisers. Some believe that the best way to placate family members who have been left out of the family business is to issue them with shares, whilst others believe that unless there are solid commercial reasons for family members to be fellow shareholders, one should avoid it if at all possible.

Where the decision has been made to introduce family members as shareholders (or even working directors), it is probably a good idea to formalise in writing the way key events will be handled. This can be done in the form of shareholders' agreements or a special written agreement between the family shareholders in what is called a 'Family Constitution'. A method of settling or arbitrating on disputes should also be included in the agreement. You might consider it helpful to include a provision in your agreement that an outside body, such as the Centre for Effective Dispute Resolution, will be called in if a deadlock is reached.

A major point on which all family business experts agree is that business and personal life must be strictly separated and spouses and relatives of the owners should be kept out of business affairs wherever possible.

THE RIGHTS OF MINORITY SHAREHOLDERS

Let us now assume that despite having considered the potential difficulties of having co-owners and despite your best efforts to raise money from outside agencies, or take on employees to fill the expertise gap, you decide to bring in a co-owner after all. It is now likely that this person will be a minority shareholder in your company.

Or, are you a minority shareholder yourself, who has been brought into a company for one of the reasons we have looked at above? Or, perhaps, you are a sleeping partner holding a minority interest in a business, or even a former 100% owner who now has individuals or institutions as the majority shareholders.

What are the rights of a minority shareholder generally and what are their particular options when it comes to planning their exit from a company?

In private companies, minority shareholders have little power or influence when it comes to making business decisions. A shareholder with 50% or more of the shares can effectively run and manage a company (and decide such things as salary levels, dividend policy, who will be the company's directors, etc.). There are other decisions that require 'special resolutions', which require a 75% voting control, but most important matters are within the power of a 50% shareholder.

Minority shareholders are entitled to certain important information, such as the company's accounts, and they can attend shareholders' meetings, but in regard to those things that are usually important to them (e.g. Will I get a dividend?) they have little influence because, in private companies dividends rely on there being a profit and profits often rely on the level of salaries, which the majority shareholder controls (unless this is covered in a shareholders' agreement).

When it comes to exiting, a minority shareholder in a private company has several problems. The most obvious one is that it is not within his power to decide that the whole business (or even a controlling interest) is for sale. So, he can only offer his minority interest. The next problem is what is a minority interest worth?

In Appendix 1 I discuss the principles of valuing a private business. The usual approach is to value the whole business and, thereafter, the value of each share. The value per share usually assumes that all the shares are for sale in one parcel and is not a value pro-rata for each share held by minority shareholders, which could be worth significantly less.

Finally, a minority shareholder will have great difficulty planning for an exit, because of the lack of control or influence I have mentioned above.

In the end, in the absence of a shareholders' agreement that protects his position and addresses his exit rights, a minority shareholder will have to rely on the goodwill of the majority shareholder if he is to receive adequate compensation when he sells his shares either alone or as part of a complete company exit.

Managing the relationship between co-owners (including the rights of minority shareholders) is heavily dependent on having a properly drawn up shareholders' agreement that addresses these issues. I will deal with shareholders' agreements in some detail in the next chapter, but in the meantime, let us return to Figure 4.1 Do I need a Business Continuity Agreement? and the other matters that arise from it.

WILLS

Moving to the right of the figure, we see that the question of having a will is important whether or not you have heirs. It goes without saying that business owners should support (or reinforce) their intentions for the disposal of their businesses with a will. If, for example, you are married and you plan to leave your business to your children and not your spouse, you should have a current will to this effect.

If you do not have a will and you die your estate will be subject to the law of intestacy. If you were not married but lived with someone (a 'partner') to whom you intended leaving assets, your partner will not be recognised under intestacy law and will have to go to court to try to become a beneficiary of your estate.

If you had intended to leave everything to your wife and made a will to this effect, but subsequently changed your mind because you had separated or divorced, it is essential that you change your will. If you are divorced it is useful to check things such as your pension and death-in-service benefits, because you would probably have named your ex-spouse as your beneficiary.

If you are a business owner and have had any turmoil in your married life it is important to have your will drawn up by an expert because, firstly your estate is unlikely to be simple and, secondly, it is possible your will could be challenged. Wills are not as simple as some would like you to believe.

PROTECTING BUSINESS ASSETS FROM DIVORCE

The next matter that arises in our figure is the question of divorce, not only of the business owner, but also of heirs.

A) DIVORCE OF A BUSINESS OWNER

You can change your will to disinherit a spouse, but if you get divorced in the meantime things are not that simple! The law on the entitlement of spouses (usually wives) to their husbands' business assets has changed dramatically in the UK over the last four years since the case of *White* v *White* and subsequent cases such as *Cowan* v *Cowan* and *Lambert* v *Lambert*. Without getting too technical, the result of these cases is that (in big-money cases at least) where a business owner is involved, spouses can expect as much as a 50:50 split of all assets following a divorce, including the value of the business. This could lead to the business owner having to sell his business; and as a judge in a recent case said: 'The time has come when the goose would have to go to market.'

So, what can a business owner do to protect a business from what could be an ill-timed and unplanned (and, consequently, disastrous) sell off? One way could be to enter into a shareholders' agreement that lays down who can own shares, as restricting ownership could help keep company shares out of the assets to be split on divorce. Also, involve outside shareholders in your business who are not related to you, so that the court has the problem of third party interests to contend with if it is considering a sale of the business.

These steps could be supported by a pre-nuptial agreement, which although not binding in the UK, could persuade the court against breaking up a business. Some experts believe that there are ways to increase the chances of a pre-nuptial agreement being accepted by the court, including updating it regularly and making reasonable provision for the spouse. Also, show that you have the ability to borrow against the business to meet your pre-nuptial obligations.

B) POTENTIAL DIVORCE OF AN HEIR

Where a business owner decides to leave business assets to an heir, he might decide that he will gift shares during his lifetime to avoid inheritance tax. The owner might, however, be concerned that the heir is married to (or is marrying) someone who is unsuitable and that the marriage will fail, resulting in the ex-husband or wife getting part of the family business. To guard against this, the business owner could place the shares in a discretionary trust, so that they are not part of the assets in a divorce. It is believed that the courts would, in most cases, look favourably on these arrangements. However, the use of trusts to defer or avoid taxation is an ever-changing aspect of the law and it is advisable to take expert advice before you make any decisions.

MANAGEMENT AND EMPLOYEES

An aspect of continuity or risk planning we have not considered is the protection of your business from the loss of key management and staff. This is, basically, an insurance-related issue. The aim of keyman insurance is to compensate the business owner for the loss of vital managers and employees both for potential loss of profits, and also for the costs of replacing them.

Key staff are often a vital part of a business's value and attractiveness to a potential purchaser, so it is prudent to have protection in place to assist you to replace them.

SUMMARY

Business Continuity Planning can be seen as part of your exit planning housekeeping. It is an activity that does not directly lead to an increase in business value, but it is a highly valuable exercise nevertheless.

We have seen in this chapter that one way to approach Business Continuity Planning is to go through a series of questions that cover your relationships with co-owners and family members. These lead to an awareness of the need to take certain steps that will protect your position in case of circumstances that could, in the absence of your actions, disrupt your business and personal life.

Business Continuity Planning is an essential part of a prudent exit plan and should begin as early as possible in your business's life. However, it needs to be constantly reviewed as your circumstances change, especially if you bring in co-owners, get married, have children or get divorced. Where you do bring in co-owners, the most important part of your planning will be to enter into a shareholders' agreement. We explain why this is so in the next chapter.

5
Shareholders' and Partnership Agreements

In the previous chapter we looked at Business Continuity Planning, including whether or not you should have co-owners in your business.

In this chapter we consider the situation where there are co-owners in a business and what should be done to arrange affairs between them to ensure there are no barriers to exit: we see that this can be achieved through having a professionally drawn up shareholders' or partnership agreement.

In summary, in this chapter we will consider the following:

- What is a shareholders' or partnership agreement?
- Why should you have a shareholders' agreement?
- Some common misconceptions about the need for a shareholders' agreement.
- Detailed contents of a shareholders' agreement for a typical SME.
- Investor and Cross-Option agreements.
- The advantages and disadvantages of having a shareholders' agreement.
- The problems that could arise if you do not have a shareholders' agreement.

INTRODUCTION

The content of this chapter could be considered by some to be rather technical. However, I do not wish the business owner to get bogged down with the technicalities and lose sight of the basic issue, namely that if you have co-owners in your business it is essential to have a shareholders' agreement, not only for the effective day-to-day running of your business, but also to ensure that you are able to execute a successful exit.

WHAT IS A SHAREHOLDERS' AGREEMENT?

A shareholders' agreement is a written agreement between the shareholders themselves and the company. A partnership agreement is a written agreement between the partners of a partnership. There is very little difference, in principle, between a shareholders' and a partnership agreement and for convenience in this chapter we will call them both shareholders' agreements, unless there is a reason to differentiate between them. Also for convenience, I will refer to shareholders and/or partners in a business as 'co-owners'.

The contents of a shareholders' agreement will differ greatly from business to business, depending on the size of the business and what the co-owners wish to include in it. By way of a simple definition, we can say that it is an agreement that covers the business relationship between co-owners and their rights and entitlements with regard to the sale of their shares or partnership equity (which we will call 'interests') and their duties and responsibilities concerning the management of the business. The parties to the agreement will often include the directors of the company who, in most SMEs, are usually also shareholders.

An agreement between co-owners which covers only the option to purchase each other's shares in the case of death or disability is known as a 'cross-option agreement' and is not, strictly speaking, a comprehensive shareholders' agreement in the sense I mean it here.

The shareholders' agreement must be compatible with the company's Articles of Association. It is usual to state in the agreement that, in the case of any conflict, the agreement will prevail. Sometimes, shareholders will amend the Articles themselves to include the extra provisions, but this is not always the preferred option as the Articles are a public document.

There are many complicated legal issues involved in shareholders' agreements and it is important that you obtain legal advice before finalising any agreement with your co-owners.

WHY SHOULD YOU HAVE A SHAREHOLDERS' AGREEMENT?

A leading lawyer said recently:

'The trouble is that when two people start-up in business they don't think they will ever fall out. But a quarter of all business partners do!'

Similarly, a leading accountant recently wrote when providing advice on a dispute between partners:

'It is very difficult to solve this problem because you do not have a shareholders' agreement. We always recommend that every company with more than one shareholder has such an agreement.'

These are reason enough to be convinced of the need for a shareholders' agreement and in Figure 5.3, below you will see others reasons why I believe a shareholders' agreement is an essential tool in exit planning where there is more than one owner in a business. But, before we consider these reasons, I would like to look at the many misconceptions that exist amongst business owners concerning the need to have a shareholders' agreement.

MISCONCEPTIONS ABOUT SHAREHOLDERS' AGREEMENTS

I list below some of the more common questions that have been asked me by business owners about shareholders' agreements and my response.

'Don't our Articles cover these issues?'

It is a common misconception amongst business owners that their Articles of Association adequately cover issues such as the pre-emptive right of shareholders to purchase shares, share transfers on death, and managerial and administrative matters between directors. With standard Articles this is simply not the case!

'Well, if they are not covered by my Articles, surely they are dealt with in the Companies or Partnership Acts?'

No, they are not. Corporate and partnership legislation provides little or no assistance in the important areas of pre-emptive rights or compulsory share transfers, or in providing guidance on disputes between partners, shareholders, or directors. The legislation is silent on most of the important practical issues and disputes that arise between business co-owners.

'I don't need a shareholders' agreement because my fellow shareholders think exactly like me – we have been close friends for years.'

This might be so, but ask yourself the following questions:

- 'If my co-owner should die tomorrow, who will inherit his shares or interests?'
- 'What will my new fellow shareholder (or partner) want to do about the running and eventual disposal of the company?'
- 'How will all this affect my ability to plan my exit in the way I wish to?'

Are you comforted by the answers?

Other questions about shareholders' agreements

There are other questions you could also ask yourself about your arrangements with co-owners within your business. For example:

- 'What are the agreements in my business for the transfer of shares in the case of disability or critical illness of a shareholder (or partner)?'

- 'Is there any funding in place to ensure that I can pay for the shares when, and if, I have an opportunity to purchase them?'

THE CONTENTS OF A SHAREHOLDERS' AGREEMENT

We will now turn to consideration of what should be included in a properly drawn up shareholders' agreement for a typical SME. This is summarised in Figure 5.1, below.

Shareholders' Agreement

A shareholders agreement should include the following provisions:

1   A general transfer of interests provision (also known as 'pre-emptive rights'), which covers the rights (or options) given to remaining owners to buy the interests of other owners who wish to leave the business and transfer or sell their interests for whatever reasons.

2   Options that are exercisable by remaining owners in the case of certain events or circumstances befalling other owners, such as death, disability, bankruptcy or retirement. (These options are known as 'cross-options' and are often contained in a separate agreement.)

3   Majority and minority shareholder protection, including 'drag-along' and 'piggyback' provisions.

4   The method of valuing the shares or interests in the various circumstances that trigger the options.

5   Mechanisms for funding the purchase of shares or interests.

6   Restraint of trade provisions (also known as 'restrictive covenants', or 'non-competition' clauses).

7   Operational or managerial provisions concerning the running of the business.

NOTES:

- In companies, certain fiduciary duties apply to directors both current and past, which could be binding despite the absence of an agreement on restraint of trade. This would not apply to shareholders who are not working in the business.

- In partnerships, in the absence of agreement for restraint of trade (or non-competition) there is no legal restraint on individuals competing against their old practice or former partners. This can have devastating effects on the goodwill value of a professional practice that is a partnership.

- Universities and investors will insist on shareholders' agreements when starting up or investing in 'spin-out' (or other start-up) companies.

Figure 5.1. Contents of a shareholders' agreement

We will now consider in more detail why these provisions are important.

THE SALE OF INTERESTS BETWEEN CO-OWNERS

This provision states that if a co-owner wishes to sell his interests (shares or share of a partnership) for any reason he must first offer those interests to his other co-owners, who have the right, but not the obligation, to purchase the interests. This is known as a 'pre-emptive right' clause and covers those circumstances where the exiting owner wishes to sell, rather than being compelled to sell because of some event (for example, becoming critically ill).

The exiting owner will either have had an offer to buy from a potential purchaser, or will desire to leave the business and, hence, would like to sell. The procedure laid down in the agreement is usually as follows:

- In the case of an external offer, the remaining co-owners have the right to purchase the interests at the same price as the offer price.
- In the case of there being no offer, the price to be paid by the remaining owners is laid down in the agreement. (How values are established in the agreement is covered below.)

'CROSS-OPTION' PROVISIONS OR AGREEMENTS

Unlike the general pre-emptive rights clause above, these provisions address the transfer of interests following certain specific events. These events usually include the death, critical illness, retirement and bankruptcy of a co-owner and the dismissal of directors who are also shareholders for specified reasons. Here the co-owner in question (or his personal representative) effectively grants an option to purchase the interests of the departing shareholder or partner at a price predetermined in the agreement.

In the case of a company, the option is given to either the company itself or other shareholders; whilst in the case of a partnership, the option is given to the other partners.

It is the occurrence of the event that 'triggers' the options and where there is any room for uncertainty care must be taken to describe the events as clearly as possible. For example, the occurrence of death and a declaration of bankruptcy are quite unambiguous, but there might be more uncertainty surrounding critical illness or the reasons for dismissal of a director. Also, it is usually necessary to distinguish between retirement at usual (stipulated) retirement age and early retirement (which itself can be for various reasons, for example illness, or desire to join another business), as different types of retirement might give rise to a different valuation of the interests of the retiring co-owner. This is covered in more detail below.

(It is usual for these 'cross-option' agreements - so called because the agreement grants each party both a 'put' and a 'call' option – to be included in separate agreements, which are usually annexed to the general shareholders' agreement.)

MINORITY AND MAJORITY PROTECTION

In Chapter 4 I talked about the difficulties minority shareholders usually have in selling their shares and the fact that parcels of minority shares often sell at a discount. Here we will look at provisions that could be included to protect majority and/or minority shareholders in a company when the business is being sold to an outside party. In the case of majority shareholder protection, the aim is to compel minority shareholders to sell their shares when the majority shareholder wishes to accept a *bona fide* offer for his shares from a third party. (This is known as a 'drag-along' provision.)

Conversely, where the majority wishes to sell, minority shareholders have the right to insist that their shares are also bought by the same purchaser at the same price per share. (This is known as a 'piggyback' provision.)

Drag-along provisions are particularly useful for dominant shareholders who have brought minority shareholders into a business, or have issued shares of the same class as their own to employees, but who still wish to be in control of their own destiny, particularly with regard to their exit. The ability to be able to sell all the shares in a private company is important because most purchasers usually wish to acquire 100% of the shares in such companies.

The piggyback provisions guard against minority shareholders being left with outside and, potentially, unsympathetic majority partners and should also ensure that a 'minority discount' is not applied to the value of the minority's shareholding.

VALUING THE DEPARTING OWNERS' INTERESTS

Many businesses with co-ownership fail to draw up shareholders' agreements, but even those with agreements in place often fail to address with any thoroughness valuation of interests being sold. This failure can result in agreements being vague and difficult to implement. The other common failure is that although the agreement contains adequate valuation methods, remaining owners make no provision for the funding of a purchase of the interests of the outgoing owners. We will now look at the valuation and funding methods that I believe business owners should consider.

A key question in the shareholders' agreement is what value will be placed on the interests of the departing co-owner. Here shareholders' and partnerships agreements can differ quite markedly, because in some partnerships (for example professional practices) no capital value is placed on the interests of incoming and outgoing partners' interests, whereas this is almost unheard of with company shares. However, despite this difference in practical approach, what follows deals with general principles and, therefore, treats companies and partnerships as being the same.

The reasons for placing a value on interests in a shareholders' agreement are, firstly, to avoid disagreement and misunderstanding amongst co-owners and, secondly, the recognition of the potential problems in negotiating a price with personal representatives, executors, or beneficiaries under a will after a co-owner has died. The method of valuation should be agreed among co-owners and clearly laid out in the agreement. This should include a method of dealing with any changes in the value of the business between the time of entering into the agreement and the events that trigger the options.

There are various commonly accepted methods that can be used to value the shares in a company or the interests in a partnership. I cover these in detail in Appendix 1 so I will not repeat myself here. The important points, however, to note are these:

1 A method of valuing the interests must be included in all agreements.

2 You should consider different valuations for the different reasons that the co-owner is leaving, or is compelled to leave.

1) Valuation methods

There is no 'right' way to value business interests, as I explain in Appendix 1 and, consequently, any number of methods can be included in a shareholders' agreement. Some of the methods that can be included and my comments on them follow below:

P/E ratio method

The widely accepted price earnings (P/E) ratio method, capitalises future maintainable earnings (or sometimes cash flow, or real profit).

I favour this method as it the one generally accepted by the business world for valuing SMEs and because it can cope with changes in value that will arise from changes in annual profitability. But, as a word of caution, this method assumes that the current appropriate capitalisation rate will remain appropriate in the future, which is a reasonable assumption in times of stable inflation, but is not so reasonable in times of economic volatility (or in volatile industries) when appropriate rates of return (and, hence, capitalisation rates) can fluctuate considerably.

A valuation by the firm's accountant's (or company's auditors) when the sale arises

The problem here is, firstly, that not all accountants are experts in business valuations and, secondly, it is open to either party to disagree with the valuation and dispute it in court.

A pre-determined amount that might be fixed in advance, or might be adjusted in line with some sort of inflation index

I consider this to be an unsatisfactory method, as values in a particular business can alter dramatically (for example, if their profits fall significantly), and often do so in the opposite direction to inflation.

An 'industry yardstick' method
This is a formula based on such things as a capitalisation of gross turnover, or gross profit, or whatever approach is accepted within the business's particular industry sector.

This approach has the advantage of simplicity and lack of ambiguity and is also a reliable indicator of value in very small businesses in relatively stable industries, but is a little simplistic in most other cases.

Periodic reviews of valuation (or new valuations) by agreement
The problem here can be that co-owners forget to, or do not bother to, complete these periodic reviews, and old values remain in the agreements.

Mutual agreement between the parties, or failing such agreement, by arbitration
Relying on such a provision usually means that co-owners end up in the law courts!

So, in summary, which method should be adopted? Personally, I favour the P/E ratio method, together with provision for periodic reviews of the capitalisation rate (probably at yearly intervals) for most businesses, because even if the co-owners overlook the reviews, this method will still provide a reasonable valuation. In some industry sectors the 'industry yardstick' method might also be acceptable. You should however, obtain specialist advice on this issue to suit your particular circumstances.

2) Different values for different exit circumstances
The key question here is whether the agreed value of a departing owner's interests should be the same in all circumstances of departure. To take an extreme example, should the agreed values be the same for when a working co-owner dies after 30 years' faithful service as for when he decides to sell out early and leave the business to join your major competitor?

As another example, remaining owners could agree, on the death of a co-owner, to pay full market value (including goodwill value) for the deceased owner's interests for moral reasons and because the funds are available through an insurance policy. But, the remaining owners could have quite a different attitude towards an owner who leaves early to take up a position with a competitor. In this case, an agreed value that reflects net tangible asset value only (or, indeed, par value only) might be considered more appropriate.

So that the agreement does not become too long-winded with many different formulas or valuation methods, it is probably a good idea to agree on one main method (such as a P/E ratio method) for some of the 'acceptable' contingencies; and to have one other, much less generous, method (for example, net tangible asset value, or even par value) for those circumstances that the business wishes to discourage (such as leaving early). This is sometimes known as the 'good leaver/bad leaver' approach to valuation.

MECHANISMS FOR FUNDING THE PURCHASE

An important part of all shareholders' agreements is a funding mechanism through which remaining owners are able to pay for the options that arise. If this is not put in place, the right to acquire interests could be difficult for remaining owners to take up and could even lead to the forced sale of the business, or of its key assets. The funding requirement should be based on a realistic and professional valuation of each co-owner's interest in the business, with a facility to vary the funding in future if the business valuation changes.

We will now look at some ways of ensuring that funds are available in the various circumstances that trigger the options to buy a departing owner's interests.

a) Death of an owner

The obvious funding mechanism here is life insurance and there are two basic ways in which policies can be set up:

- The co-owners can insure each other (that is, they are each the beneficiaries of the others' policies).
- In the case of a company, the owners can be insured by the company, which will buy back and cancel the deceased owner's shares.

Other funding methods could be savings plans, pension funds or sinking funds. The problem with this approach is that it is difficult to plan with any precision, as there is no knowing when a death will occur.

b) Critical illness of an owner

Once again, insurance is the obvious funding mechanism for this circumstance, although high premium costs could be a limiting factor. Most insurance companies link death and critical illness in one policy and the beneficiaries could be either the co-owners or, in the case of a company, the company itself. The policy will be taken out in accordance with a cross-option agreement, mentioned above.

c) Early retirement

Where there is early retirement not brought on by ill health or injury or death, insurance does not usually provide remaining co-owners with cover, so it is generally difficult to fund for this eventuality. Also, it is not usually in the interests of the business to encourage early retirement amongst co-owners and, for this reason, shareholders' agreements often state that early retirees will not receive full market value for their interests on retirement.

d) Normal retirement (i.e. at a stipulated retirement age)

Pension or savings plans can be employed if there is sufficient time available before retirement age and adequate forward planning has taken place. Otherwise, arrangements similar to early retirement (but, perhaps, with a payout more favourable to the retiree) can be entered into. Again this is a matter of policy for the co-owners to decide having received competent advice.

MANAGEMENT OR OPERATIONAL PROVISIONS

a) General provisions

This part of the agreement does not deal with the sale or transfer of interests: rather it seeks to regulate the way a business is run. It only impacts on exit planning to the extent that anything that detracts from the smooth running of the business and, consequently, its profitability is to be avoided, so I will deal with it only briefly. These general provisions cover such things as:

- Initial capital and working capital contributions.
- Directors' responsibilities and spending limits.
- Requirement for board approvals.
- Investment and dividend policy.
- Retirement policy.
- Treatment of 'key persons' and funding for their loss.
- Course of action in case of disagreement between co-owners on major matters, including agreement to wind up and method of winding up.

This part of the agreement could also address circumstances that could cause disruption to the business and to the exit strategy planning process. Examples of these are:

- Professional negligence by co-owners.
- Liabilities as a result of co-owner being a director or officer of another company.
- Infidelity of officers and employees.

b) Restraint of trade (restrictive covenants, or non-competition clauses)

Restraint of trade provisions directly influence exit planning, as their purpose is to protect business value and, hence, exit value. They aim to restrict competition from co-owners and working directors who leave the business. The provisions should be specific in terms of the time period and geographic area and are usually restricted to the same type of business or industry as the subject business.

It is a basic rule of English law that all restraints of trade are void unless they can be justified as being reasonable. Another fundamental principal of the law is that you cannot prevent someone from earning a living. A restraint must, therefore, afford the party who has sought it no more than adequate protection for the interest he is entitled to protect. In practice it is harder to try to prevent an employee from working for a competitor than preventing an owner or director from using the information gathered whilst in your business to compete against you, or to entice away your customers or employees.

Where restraint of trade could be vital, is in the area of professional partnership competition. Without such an agreement, the value of goodwill for the whole practice could be in doubt and, therefore, so could the value of individual partners' equity. This could be particularly damaging to newer partners because they do not have the direct personal contact with a large number of the firm's clients and, therefore, no way of protecting their own goodwill (by keeping clients) should the practice dissolve and cease to trade.

INVESTOR AGREEMENTS

Where a business is set up with outside investors, or where outsiders, such as venture capitalists (VCs), invest in a business in its early stages of growth, it is usual for the investors to insist on entering into a shareholders' agreement with the founder owners. A good example of this is 'spin out' companies, where scientists and inventors at universities, or in industry create businesses to exploit their technological or scientific inventions or discoveries.

As the investors hold most of the cards and many founder/owners have little commercial experience, the shareholders' agreements negotiations are usually somewhat one-sided. So, what can founders of fledgling companies do to protect themselves when they are in a comparatively weak bargaining position?

In short, I believe that you should be prepared by securing expert advice and familiarising yourself with the content of standard agreements, if possible. In this way, you should be able to secure more favourable terms, particularly with regard to minority protection, including the 'piggyback' provisions.

WHEN SHOULD I ENTER INTO A SHAREHOLDERS' AGREEMENT?

THE STORY OF THE SHAREHOLDERS' HUSBAND

'Yes,' you say, 'I'm sure these sorts of problems happen to some people who don't have shareholders' agreements, but in my case it's different, because I have known and worked with my minority shareholder for 25 years, and he will agree with whatever I want to do with regard to the transfer of shares, or the sale of the whole business.'

In response I will tell you a brief story. A husband and wife in their late 50s (who I will call Derrick and Anne) approached me to help them plan their exit. They had built up a very successful nursery and garden centre business in the North of England. The business was owned by a limited company of which they owned 80% of the shares, having sold 20% of the shares on very favourable terms to their administration manager, who I will call Sue. There was no shareholders' agreement in place.

They wished to exit from the business in three years. I pointed out to them the problem that could arise with Sue if she did not want to sell her shares, because purchasers of private companies usually wish to buy 100% of a company. I got a response just like the one mentioned above to the effect that there would be no problem with Sue, who always did what they wished. I asked them to talk to Sue about their plans to exit and to suggest that to formalise matters they should enter into a shareholders' agreement.

Two weeks later I got a telephone call from Derrick in a rather distressed state who told me that he had just heard back from Sue to the effect that her husband had advised her not to agree to sell her shares and not to enter into any agreement!

You can imagine that, without resolution of this issue, exit planning with any certainty would be very difficult for Derrick and Anne.

This little story highlights at least four lessons:

1   The falacy of the idea that something bad only happens to other people.

2   The fact that when dealing with people you never know what they really think, or what they will do when the crunch comes.

3   That in business dealings it is not only the principal person you need to be concerned about, but also their relatives or partners who have influence over them.

4   Probably most importantly of all, that if the shareholders' agreement had been suggested when the shares were first issued on favourable

terms to Sue, the problem would have never have arisen, because she would have been only too pleased to co-operate.

SUMMARY

The advantages of agreements between co-owners that facilitate an exit strategy and provide peace of mind are now, hopefully, obvious to you as a business owner. However, by way of a summary, Figure 5.2, below lists the reasons why, when you have co-owners in your business, you should have a shareholders' agreement.

- It ensures that shares and business interests pass smoothly between owners in all circumstances in which an owner wishes to exit.
- It ensures that business interests do not end up in strange or hostile hands.
- It addresses what will happen to interests when various events take place, such as the death, critical illness, bankruptcy, early retirement, or dismissal of one of the co-owners.
- It ensures the business need not be wound up upon the occurrence of one of the events mentioned above.
- It ensures the continuation of the business without prolonged interruption or loss of momentum, enabling surviving co-owners to assume control of the business as a going concern with equipment, employees, customers, goodwill, etc., intact.
- In the event of death, the deceased co-owner's estate can be settled promptly and efficiently with no undue delays caused by difficulties encountered in the disposal of an interest in the business.
- The outgoing co-owner or his estate is free from the fear of being completely dependent upon the fortunes and skills of the surviving co-owners.
- It overcomes the emotional and practical problems associated with negotiations having to be entered into with, for example, the widow (or personal representative) of a deceased co-owner at the time when she will be most distraught.
- In the event of death, the deceased co-owner's estate can be relieved of the worries and responsibilities in connection with the

business, more so if the agreement enables the estate to obtain a release from personal guarantees.

- It allows for the co-owner to plan with the knowledge that he can expect to receive a just and fair price for his interest in the business.

- By ensuring its continuation, a business can engender confidence in its employees, creditors and bankers.

- It ensures a guaranteed market for the outgoing or deceased co-owner's interest in the business at a pre-agreed price.

- By clearly defining operating rights and obligations of all parties to the arrangement, it assists in the elimination of any potential friction between the parties.

- For outgoing co-owners, the aim of exit planning should be to establish a market for their interests and to optimise their exit price. A well-drafted shareholder's agreement can achieve this on a co-owner's retirement by confirming who the buyers are (that is, the remaining co-owners); establishing the price (through the agreed methods of valuation of interests); and providing the buyers with the means by which the price can be paid (for example, through insurance, etc.).

- In other words, a carefully structured Business Continuity Plan built around a shareholders' agreement could be the only exit strategy plan available to an outgoing co-owner: but it could be the perfect plan!

- From the remaining co-owners' point of view, a shareholders' agreement could ensure that the business remains in their hands, provides a mechanism for establishing an agreed selling price and, hopefully, puts in place the means to pay for their acquisition.

Figure 5.2. Why have a shareholders' agreement?

Figure 5.3, below looks at the question of having a shareholders' agreement from a slightly different angle and summarises the problems that could arise if you do not have one.

Where you do not have a shareholders' agreement, the following problems could occur in your business:

1   The departing or deceased co-owners (or their executors) may:

- demand an unreasonable price for their interests in the business from the remaining co-owners, resulting in disputes and legal action;

- wish to sell their interests to potentially hostile, or totally unsuitable, third parties;

- demand immediate repayment of loans and other amounts due to them, which the other co-owners cannot pay immediately.

2   In professional partnerships where there is no restraint of trade agreement, the goodwill value of the practice (and, therefore, the goodwill value of each partner's share of the practice) can be worthless when a key partner leaves and is able to go into competition with the practice. This can have disastrous results for partners who have purchased goodwill in the practice and hoped to retrieve this capital on leaving the partnership.

3   In private companies, shareholders are often working directors who can have gained specialist knowledge whilst in the employ of the company. Their departure can cause considerable damage to the company unless they are prevented by agreement from competing against the company.

4   Disputes, or legal action among co-owners could lead to adverse publicity for the business and to creditors calling for immediate payment of accounts, or to banks discontinuing credit or calling in loans, or to employees being unsettled and even leaving; all of which could have a negative effect on the business.

5   In the case of a divorce of a shareholder (including either the husband and wife owners, or minority shareholders such as grown children in a family company) a shareholder's equity could fall into hostile hands, unless there is agreement on who is able to own shares or what they are worth. This could lead to a forced sale of the company to resolve a stalemate.

6   Majority shareholders may be restrained from accepting an attractive offer for all of a company's shares from a *bona fide* third party purchaser because minority shareholders refuse to sell, or are holding out for a higher price.

Figure 5.3. Problems of not having a shareholders' agreement.

6

What are your exit options?

Choosing the optimum exit option (or method of exit) for your business is a key part of exit planning. Ideally, you should have considered how you were going to exit when you started (or acquired) your business, but I know from experience that many business owners do not even think about exit until very late on in their business lives and that when they do think about an exit option they consider only a trade sale.

After reading this chapter you will realise that there are many possible ways of exiting a business. Having decided what method is likely to be the best for you, you should tailor (or groom) your business's development and growth with this exit in mind.

In this chapter we will:

- look at what we mean by an 'optimum' exit option;
- examine briefly the various exit options available to the owner of a private business so that you are able to form some initial views on the options that could be relevant to your business.

This should prepare you for the next chapter when we consider how you can choose the optimum exit option for your business.

WHAT DO WE MEAN BY 'THE OPTIMUM EXIT OPTION'?

Most business owners seek to get the best results from their exit. This involves achieving some of the following outcomes:

- To receive the maximum gross selling price.

- To pay as little tax as legally possible on the sale proceeds.
- To transfer business assets to heirs or loved ones.
- To pass on the business to work colleagues or partners.
- To receive sufficient money to retire comfortably.
- To see their business name and reputation continue.

Which of these outcomes are the most important to you will, of course, be a matter of personal choice. However, from my work with private business owners, I have found that most believe that maximising their net exit price is the first priority and one which will take care of most of the other objectives. For business owners with family members working in the business, many were more concerned about a tax effective transfer of the business to family members than merely maximising their exit price. For the purposes of this book, therefore, our definition of 'the optimum exit option' is the method of exit that maximises the owner's net exit proceeds and/or personal satisfaction.

CHOICE OF OPTION COULD BE CRUCIAL

It is important to realise that the choice of the optimum exit option (and the subsequent proper grooming of your business for disposal through this method) is not necessarily just about the quantum (or amount) of money you will receive on disposal: it could make the difference between disposing of the business for a fair price and not being able to dispose of it at all.

With the choice of the right option you could be creating a market for your equity that did not exist previously. An example of this could be where you have previously failed to generate any outside interest through a trade sale, which leads you to groom a senior manager with a view to a management buy-out that you agree to partly fund.

WHAT ARE THE EXIT OPTIONS?

There are many ways in which you can dispose of your business. The most common ones are listed in Figure 6.1, below. There are also several variations of these. An example of a variation is where in a trade sale you sell only part of your shares rather than all of them. Another example is where in a management buy-out an outside CEO is brought in to assist the internal management, making it partly a buy-out and partly a buy-in.

The main exit options available to a private business owner are as follows:

1 Transferring a business to family members, known as a 'family succession'.

2 Sale to a third party, known as a 'trade sale'.

3 Sale to internal management, known as a management buy-out or 'MBO'. (Note an important variation of this is a sale to employees.)

4 Sale to outside management, known as a management buy-in, or 'MBI'.

5 A sale to your employees, known as an employee buy-out, or 'EBO'.

6 A public listing on the stock exchange, also known as a 'flotation'.

7 Initially franchising your business operations and, as a second stage, selling the franchisor business.

8 Merger of smaller businesses or sole traders in the same industry, sometimes known as a 'sole trader merger'.

9 Ceasing to trade and ultimate liquidation, or a managed close down.

Figure 6.1. The most common exit options for SMEs.

THE EXIT OPTIONS EXPLAINED IN BRIEF

In the next chapter we look at how you can choose the optimum exit option for your business. We suggest you begin by making a short list of the ones that, on the face of it, appear to be relevant before making your final decision. To make even a short list, however, it is obviously helpful if you understand how the various options work. Below we provide a brief review of the options from the perspective of how they might be applicable to your business.

(A fuller explanation of all these exit options can be seen in my book *Exit Strategy Planning: Grooming your business for sale or succession*, published by Gower Publishing Limited.)

1 FAMILY SUCCESSION

A family succession involves passing on your business to a family member. Most private business owners with children, or who have a close relationship with a younger relative, would like to go down this route if possible. Unfortunately, even those with close relatives such as children, often find that their heirs are not interested in, or capable of, taking over the running of the family business.

Although desirable from the point of view of personal satisfaction for the owner, family succession can be the most difficult exit strategy of all. The greatest problems are that family and business goals and cultures often clash, objectivity is often absent and emotion rather than business practicality takes over.

The other major issue with family succession is the time and effort needed to prepare an heir for the task of owning and running a business. This is usually accomplished through a five-stage process of:

1   *Learning* the business operations.

2   *Doing*: that is partaking in all aspects of the business's operations.

3   *Managing* all aspects of the business.

4   *Leading* other managers as a preparation for running the business.

5   *Outside experience*, which can be undertaken at any time during the grooming process.

As you can see, the successful grooming of an heir could take many years and should start early in the prospective heir's business life. I would advise those owners considering this path to set aside at least 10 (and preferably 15) years for the task.

(You can read more about choosing and training your heir in Chapter 9: Tailoring your business to fit your exit.)

2 A TRADE SALE

A sale to a third party on the open market (known as a 'trade sale') is the method of disposal most private business owners think of when they consider disposing of their businesses, and it is still the way most private businesses are sold. Most businesses in most industry sectors are suitable for a trade sale and there are usually no special attributes that the owner or the business need if it is to be disposed of through this route.

The key question that an owner should ask when considering a trade sale is:

'Is this the best way for me to maximise my financial return (and, perhaps, my personal satisfaction) when exiting my business, or should I be thinking of different options?'

A general understanding of all the main exit options available to you will help you to answer this question with authority. If, having achieved this understanding by reading this chapter, you still believe that a trade sale is the optimum exit option for your business you should then look into this method in more detail. For this I can recommend *Selling your Business for all it's Worth*, by Mark Blayney, published by How to Books Ltd.

As most businesses are suitable for a trade sale, the issues that need considering are often more to do with your own financial position than the position of your business. Some of these issues are discussed below.

a) The value of your business

The value at which you dispose of your interests is central to any exit option. In some processes, such as a public listing, you will receive expert advice on your business's probable value. In others, such as an MBO, the value could be worked out between buyer and seller. In a trade sale, however, the seller usually needs to set an asking price upfront and has to rely on his own judgement, or that of his advisers, to establish the amount. This is a problem for most business owners because neither they nor their accountants are usually business valuation experts.

Where you fix your own price for your business in a trade sale you must bear in mind that the price at which the business is listed for sale (that is the asking price) often determines how quickly the business will be sold and/or whether it will be sold or not, because:

- although all prices are negotiable and business people expect to haggle, if you start with a price that is far too high, potential purchasers are unlikely even to begin the first stages of negotiating;

- you will have started off with unreasonable expectations and will find it hard to accept what might, in the event, be a reasonable market price.

It is better to face up to what your business is really worth at the beginning, rather than going through the costly and stressful business of trying to sell a business that is over-priced. Think carefully about market value based on sound valuation principles and not subjective issues like 'this business owes me the best years of my life.'

You will get a better idea of how to value your business once you have read Appendix 1. You should also seek professional advice from a reputable business valuer. Make your decision on an asking price for your business once you have all the relevant facts and received outside advice.

b) Getting your price

An important part of any exit is to ensure you achieve your asking price. With a trade sale three issues are relevant, namely: vendor finance, retentions and 'earn-outs'. We will now look at these briefly in turn. I deal with these matters in more detail in Chapter 12.

Vendor finance

It is sometimes difficult for purchasers of a small business to borrow money to finance their purchase (particularly where goodwill value is a major part of the price), unless they can provide security outside the business, such as a house that still has some clear equity value.

One way of overcoming this difficulty and still achieving your asking price would be for you to provide vendor finance. This is an issue that requires careful thought by the vendor.

Retentions

In a trade sale of a small business it is not unusual for a purchaser to keep back a specified portion of the purchase price until it is proved that the business can retain its customers or clients, (i.e. its turnover or sales levels). The withheld portion of the purchase price is called a 'retention'. It will usually be held in trust until the trial period has expired. When the performance conditions are met the retention is paid to the vendor.

'Earn-outs'

An 'earn-out' is different from a retention in that it refers to the circumstance where the ultimate purchase consideration is based strictly on a multiple of future earnings achieved by the business (and can go up or down); whereas with a retention the price is set beforehand, but the full amount is only paid when and if profit or turnover targets are met.

You will need to consider whether either a retention or an earn-out provision is likely to be requested by the purchaser and what your reaction to this will be. Your response is likely to depend on whether you need the entire sale proceeds immediately.

c) Selling the business yourself?

You can sell your business through a business transfer agent (company broker), or you could decide to handle the sale yourself. If you decide to handle the sale yourself, you should address the following questions:

- Am I able to establish a fair market price for my business?
- Will I be able to put together an attractive memorandum of offer document?
- Will I be able to find someone who wishes to buy my business?
- How do I best structure the sale transaction?
- Am I in a position to provide some of the funding?
- How do I arrange a suitable handover and how long should this be for?
- If I want to continue to be involved in the business after sale (perhaps as a consultant), how do I go about this?

3 MANAGEMENT BUY-OUTS (MBOS)

a) What is an MBO?

An MBO is a business sale where the buyers are the management of the business. Contrary to common belief, an MBO is an exit option available to any private business and not just the larger ones; nor is it necessary to have Venture Capitalists (VCs), corporate finance specialists, or banks involved, but as MBOs usually need outside funding, financiers of one sort or another usually play a part in the process.

b) Advantages of an MBO as an exit option

Assuming you have suitably talented management in your business that you believe would be interested in an MBO, an MBO could be the optimum exit option for you. Your management could be the perfect buyers of your business for the reasons listed in Figure 6.2, below.

- Management should be aware of the potential of the business and, because they understand its operations better than any outside buyer, they should have sensible ideas of how to achieve this potential.
- Management is familiar with the business clients, suppliers, financiers and employees.
- As an owner, you know your management and their capabilities intimately and, hopefully, you trust them.
- With a sale to a group of people you know well you are more likely to be able to structure the sale to suit your retirement planning needs (including your possible future involvement in the business) than in other disposal options.
- There is a great deal of personal satisfaction in seeing people you have taught, worked with, know and like, purchase your business.
- Management is often driven by personal and emotional reasons to buy your business, making them keener to buy than most outside buyers and, perhaps, to pay you more for it.

Figure 6.2. Why management could be the perfect buyer.

c) Does your business qualify for an MBO?

The first step in answering this question is to establish whether the MBO needs outside finance, or whether the management can fund it with their own resources. Where the management does not need outside financial help, any business can qualify for an MBO.

Where management does need outside financial help, the general requirements of suitability of a business for an MBO are the same regardless of its size, but size will determine what sort of outside investors are likely to be interested, because VCs are unlikely to be interested in a deal in which they are investing less than £500000. The general requirements of suitability can be summarised as a strong cash flow and management expertise.

Strong cash flow

Business managers are not usually wealthy and, consequently, they will need to borrow a large portion of the purchase price if they are to undertake a successful buy-out. This will result in a substantial interest bill and, consequently, the business will need to have a steady, positive cash flow to meet its repayments schedule and working capital requirements, including reasonable salaries for the managers themselves. If the management is put under too much financial pressure, the business itself will suffer and could be in danger of collapse. If you, as vendor, are part of the financing arrangements through providing vendor finance, this will, of course, also put your own position at risk.

The suitability of the cash flow to finance the transaction has to be established with rigorous, professionally produced cash flow forecasts.

Management expertise

It is usual for an MBO to be a team effort, with senior managers, a CEO and financiers making up the team. At the head of the team should be an effective, experienced CEO who has the right leadership qualities and good relations with the rest of the team. The management team should include members who have a wide range of business skills. Where the MBO is being financed from outside, the managers must have the confidence of the financiers and the ability to talk their language.

Generally speaking, the management should have the following attributes:

- Experience in the essential operational functions of the business.
- Strong financial management skills.
- Involvement in day-to-day running of the business in a hands-on way.
- Ability to produce well thought-out strategic and business plans, with accurate financial forecasts.

Where outside management is brought into the team, the transaction becomes a Management Buy-in, which we discuss next.

4 MANAGEMENT BUY-INS (MBIs)

An MBI is an MBO in which outside management (sometimes one person with particular talents) puts a team together to purchase a business from the owner. Where an individual is brought in by the financiers to bolster a management team that has perceived management weaknesses, this is a hybrid transaction called an MBO/MBI or BIMBO. A further variation on this is where an institution initiates and drives the buy-out (called an Institutional Buy-out, or IBO).

The prerequisites of a business for an MBI transaction are the same as for an MBO (except, of course, for the make up of the management team). As a business owner if you feel that your business is suitable for a management buyout, but that there are weaknesses in the current management team, you could try to find a suitable outside party as the potential CEO to lead a buy-out team. On the other hand, potential CEOs from outside the business could recognise an opportunity in your business and themselves initiate a buy-in with the support of outside financiers.

5 SELLING TO YOUR EMPLOYEES

The process of selling to employees is very similar to an MBO and the qualities of the business to qualify for an employee buy-out (EBO) are more or less the same as those for an MBO. But there are some differences.

The first difference is that the buyers are the whole, or most of, the work force. This means that a decision to buy needs to be made, theoretically, by a large number of people.

It is unlikely that the employees could fund an EBO themselves, so most EBOs need to have the support of a specialist EBO financier. Financiers specialising in backing EBOs are a relatively new phenomenon in the UK, but are growing in importance. They work to a fairly strict formula, which usually involves all employees receiving a token free entitlement of shares, whilst having the option to buy more. This means all employees participate in the buy-out whilst eliminating the difficulty of getting all the employees to agree the purchase and the price. Everyone is in from the beginning and those who are keen to invest further may do so. Some employees will become senior managers and even directors, while the former owners may stay on for some time to assist in the transition process.

The bulk of the finance is usually debt provided by the specialist EBO financier, so the business needs to be able to support a high level of borrowings: another reason why the former owners might be persuaded to stay on. For the owners, there could be a considerable amount of satisfaction knowing that employees are able to share in the future profits of the business. As one owner recently said to me:

'We had been thinking of selling for some time. I wanted to be financially secure when I sold out, but at the same time I wanted to be able to look my employees in the eye and know that I hadn't sold them down the river.'

6 PUBLIC LISTING, OR FLOTATION

Most private businesses do not have the profit history or potential, nor do they have the capital value to qualify for the minimum listing requirements of the Main or Alternative boards of the London Stock Exchange (LSE). Also, City investors are wary of family companies that wish to list, but also want to retain ownership of a large majority of their company's shares.

However, despite these apparent problems, some private companies still have the chance of a public listing, because the Listing Rules are not hard and fast and because City investors will be attracted to well priced investments with good prospects, be they 'family companies' or not. Indeed, for some small companies (such as high-tech start-ups) flotation will be the prime exit strategy.

In certain phases of the economic cycle, investor requirements are more biased towards entrepreneurial enterprises, and profit potential (rather than an actual profit history) could be enough to attract investor support for a flotation. Also, the LSE rules for the Alternative Investment Market (AIM) are not as strict as for the main board. In addition, alternative exchanges with less structured rules, such as OFEX, exist for smaller companies, although it should be noted that at the time of writing (2004) the OFEX exchange is in some financial trouble itself.

When considering exit, you should accept that a flotation is a long-term (or multi-staged) strategy. The first stage is an initial sale of your equity to the public, whilst the further stages could involve the sale of further tranches of shares into a much more liquid market and at, hopefully, ever-increasing prices (depending on how well your business is doing). A flotation can be a high reward strategy and if you have a profitable business with strong growth potential you should give it serious consideration.

To be listed on the LSE, either on the AIM or the Main Board, a company needs to meet certain minimum requirements. Full details of these requirements are available from the exchanges concerned. It is worth noting that the AIM is currently growing much more strongly than the Main Board, because of its lower costs and easier regulatory regime.

Finally, you should be aware that besides the difficulty that small businesses have in attracting institutional support, the costs of flotation for a small company are very high (especially when considered as a percentage of total capital raised) and this, together with the amount of time and risk involved, makes flotation an unlikely exit for most small businesses.

7 FRANCHISING

Like a flotation, franchising your business could be a multi-staged exit strategy. The first stage would be to establish a franchise business by selling off part of your current business operations as franchises. Next you could establish further franchise outlets and, eventually, you could dispose of the franchisor business itself.

If you are thinking about franchising your business as an exit option, you should check initially whether your business might be suitable. Figure 6.3 below, lists the characteristics necessary for a business to be suitable for franchising.

To be suitable for franchising a business should have the following characteristics:

- It must have strong brand recognition, or to be able to build one.
- It must have a unique or new way of conducting business (that is, a unique operating system), or an aspect of its business that is unique, such as a formula, or patent.
- The business system must be relatively simple and be able to be taught to others, so that suitable franchisees can be found and trained.
- It must be able to duplicate its operations outside of its current

geographical areas of operation.

- There must be sufficient gross margin in the business for the franchisee to pay the franchise fees and still make a reasonable net profit.

- The business must have financial and operational systems in place that can keep track of the franchisees' operations and ensure that the franchisor gets paid.

From the personal point of view, you the owner must be capable of managing a group of independently-minded business people who will make up your franchisees.

Figure 6.3. Suitable charactersitics for franchising.

Full assistance on setting up or acquiring a franchise can be obtained from the British Franchise Association.

8 SMALL BUSINESS OR SOLE TRADER MERGERS

The mergers we are considering here are those between smaller private businesses and professional practices who are, typically, sole traders. This exit option allows a retiring business owner to plan an exit strategy at an early stage through an arrangement with another owner, who is keen to expand his business. For the retiring owner this can be a relatively low risk option and allows you some latitude in working out your retirement at a reduced level of intensity in the new merged business.

The sole trader merger can be a three-staged exit strategy, as follows:

- Stage one involves the merger of two businesses (with perhaps an initial purchase of equity).
- Stage two involves the buy out of the older owner's interest (or the balance of his interests) in the merged business by the younger owner.
- Stage three could involve the retiring owner working out a retirement period as an employee in the merged entity.

To consider exiting through this method you would, typically, be a sole trader and you would need to find a younger sole trader in the same industry with a similar working philosophy to your own. (I discuss this exit option in more detail in Appendix 2.)

9 CEASING TO TRADE (A MANAGED CLOSE DOWN)

If going-concern status is not maintained, most businesses will lose a large part of their value. Experience shows that when assets such as plant and equipment and/or stock are sold in auctions (or in 'fire sales') they seldom fetch their so-called 'market value' and often sell for less than their written down value. Even real property can fail to reach market value when it is sold too quickly without the proper advertising. Also, a business that has lost its going-concern status will usually lose its goodwill value.

To close down your business operations first and then attempt to sell off its assets is, usually, the worst of all exit options for you. However, there are circumstances where the value of the business as a going-concern is no greater than the value of its assets and, indeed, where the value of the assets could exceed going-concern business value. It is in these circumstances that an orderly disposal of a solvent company's assets followed by a formal liquidation of the company could make financial sense. To explain this more fully we will now look at two examples:

Example 1: Where the value of the business as a going concern is less than the value of its assets

The best way to explain this is to put figures to the example. Assume that an earth moving business makes an after-tax profit of £500000 and the industry standard is to value it by applying a P/E ratio of six. Let us assume also that the plant and equipment on its books has a written down value of £4.5 million (and this reflects reasonable market value) and other assets and liabilities cancel each other out, thus giving the business a total net asset value of £4.5 million.

The business has a going-concern value of, and is likely to sell for, a price of £3 million, whilst its net asset value is £4.5 million. Assuming that the owners do not have sufficient time to build up business profitability (and going-concern value) before exiting, they could approach this dilemma in one of two ways, namely:

1   Where all the assets are not necessary for the production of the business's income, surplus assets could be sold separately from the business in an attempt to achieve the £4.5 million price.

2   Where the business does utilise all its assets to generate its income, the

assets themselves could be sold and the business closed down.

Example 2: Where the value of the business is no greater than the value of the assets

This can arise in the following circumstances:

1   Where a business's ability to earn an income is totally reliant on the owner's personal skills and experience, so that when he or she leaves the business it has no going-concern (or goodwill) value over and above what can be realised for its assets.

2   The business is in an industry that has no economic future, because of such things as changes to laws or regulations, or other macro-economic circumstances and, consequently, it has no value as a business *per se*.

3   Regardless of all the owner's attempts, the business cannot be disposed of and the owner is forced to sell off the assets.

Sometimes, the close down of your business will not be of your choosing. If you are forced through insolvency to put your business into administration or liquidation then planning for your exit is probably completely out of your hands. In these circumstances you would need to seek expert legal advice.

Also, before the company sells off its assets, you should get expert tax advice on the question of how best to transfer the cash proceeds of asset sales from the company to its owners.

SUMMARY

Choosing the optimum exit strategy is a key step in exit planning. However, many private business owners are not aware of the various exit options available to them.

This chapter has briefly analysed the most common exit options so that you are better able to understand how they work. These options are:

- A family succession.
- A trade sale.
- A management buy-out, or MBO.
- A management buy-in, or MBI.
- An employee buy-out, or EBO.
- A public listing.
- Franchising, as a two-staged exit.
- A sole trader merger.
- A managed close down.

You should now be in a position to consider, in general terms, which option is the one that best suits your business and personal circumstances. In the next chapter we will show you how you can choose the optimum exit option.

7

How to choose the optimum
exit option

In this chapter we show you how to choose the optimum exit option for your business. You do this by going through the following steps:

- Thinking about which option is likely to maximise your disposal price and give you the greatest personal satisfaction.

- Going through an options-elimination worksheet, which will help you identify those options that are not relevant to your business.

- Arriving at a theoretical short list from which, eventually, you will make your final choice.

- Deciding on your final exit option after consideration of the possible impact of your decision on third parties, such as family members, employees, customers and suppliers.

ESTABLISHING THE ALTERNATIVES:
AN OVERVIEW

Having addressed the structural and timing issues covered earlier in this book, the next step in planning your exit involves choosing the best exit option. This involves choosing the option that will maximise the value of your equity and be the most favourable from your financial planning and personal satisfaction point of view.

For some owners, the choice of exit option could be dependent solely on a strong personal preference or need, which makes it easy to eliminate those exit options that are not compatible with this preference or need. For example, if your desire is to leave your business to your daughter, you will not be considering other exit options, even if you believe they will probably result in a larger exit price, or other personal advantages to you. This elimination on the basis of a strong preference could leave you a favoured first choice, which you plan to implement if possible. Only if this option does not work out (for example, because your daughter proves unable to run the business), would you then consider other options.

However, for most owners the choice of an exit option should be based on wider considerations and should involve an examination of all the possible exit options available before arriving at a short list. How this can be done is the subject of this chapter.

OWNER'S PERSONAL PREFERENCES AND NEEDS

Where an owner has children, or other family members who could take over the business, it is usual for him or her to wish to pass on the business to a family member. Where this is not possible, or where the owner has no immediate heirs, some owners would prefer to sell the business to co-owners, or to their management and employees.

There are, of course other exit options to consider and in Figure 7.1 below, we look at the advantages and disadvantages of each exit option in general terms.

This figure considers the options in terms of:

- *Value*: whether the option chosen is likely to achieve the maximum value to the owner.
- *Risk*: the degree of risk involved in bringing the disposal transaction to fruition.
- *Control*: the amount of control the owner is likely to have over the running and the management of the business after the sale.
- *Personal financial planning*: does the transaction assist in the personal financial planning of the owner, or can it be structured to assist this planning?
- *Payment risk*: the likelihood of the seller being paid the total purchase price.

	Can I achieve maximum value?	What is the risk factor in disposal?	Can I retain control after sale?	Will this be good for my personal financial planning?	Will I be assured payment?	Will I have deal flexibility?	What should my personal satisfaction be?
Family Succession	sometimes	moderate	probably	yes	no	yes: a lot	very high
Employees or managers (MBO/MBI)	yes	moderate	probably not	yes	depends on terms	limited amount	moderate to high
Sole trader merger	yes	moderate	some	yes	yes	yes: some	moderate
Trade sale	yes	low	no	depends on timing	depends on terms	probably not	moderate to low
Public listing	yes	high	some	yes	yes for initial offering	no	high
Franchising	yes	moderate to high	yes: of franchisor business	yes	no	yes	high
Managed close-down	no	low	no	probably not	yes	no	low
Liquidation – fire sale	definitely not	low	no	no	yes	no	very low

Figure 7.1. Exit options: initial assessment.

- *Deal flexibility*: the amount of flexibility that the transaction provides to the owner, including payment terms and working in the business in some capacity after sale.
- *Personal satisfaction*: how much satisfaction (other than financial) is the owner likely to derive from the transaction?

For example, a family succession provides the owner with a great deal of flexibility on how the deal is structured and his ability to work in and exercise influence in the business after sale. It also provides a large amount of personal satisfaction but, probably, at the expense of receiving the maximum sale price.

Conversely, a trade sale could achieve the maximum sale price, but provide no way of continuing in the business after sale (say, as a consultant) and may even be to a hated competitor, which will probably give the owner no personal satisfaction at all!

Some of the considerations in Figure 7.1 are subjective and will not reflect your own views. The vital thing for you is whether your preferred option is practical and relevant to your business and your personal circumstances.

OPTIONS ELIMINATION

For those of you who start with no preconceived exit preferences and an open mind about exit options, The Options Elimination Worksheet (Figure 7.2) is designed to help in the initial process of sifting out those exit options that are unsuitable or impractical for your particular business circumstances. Once you have eliminated the unsuitable options it will be easier for you to decide on the best option from the remaining ones.

Remember, you are not only choosing the best option for current economic circumstances or for your business's current situation, but also what is possible in future with planning. This is why how successful you are in implementing your plans as well as the possible state of the economy and your industry at the proposed disposal date, will be so important.

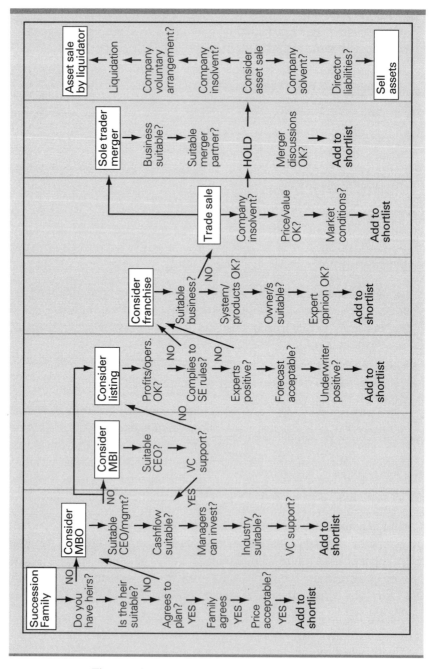

Figure 7.2. Exit options: elimination worksheet.

OPTIONS ELIMINATION: HOW TO USE THE WORKSHEET

The worksheet lists from left to right the various exit options available to private business owners in what could be considered as an order of personal preference. We suggest that you work through the worksheet from the top left hand corner, considering each question until you come to a negative, and then move to the right to the next option, until you arrive at an option that seems possible for your business. We start with the possibility of family succession.

Family succession

If you have heir/s you should explore this option first. The crucial first question is how suitable one or more of them is for the task of owning and running the business. If the answer to either of these questions is negative you cannot proceed with this option and you will need to consider your next option, namely an MBO.

Should you believe that there is an heir available who is suitable, you can then proceed to the next stage of elimination: that is, does the heir agree with your plan? We suggest you then put the plan to other family members to see whether they agree. You continue with the elimination process until you come up with a 'NO' answer, which forces you to move right to the next option.

Should all answers be 'YES', this option is now a theoretical possibility and should be added to your short list of possible exit options.

Management Buy-Out (MBO)

The first question here is whether a suitable leader exists in the business (who is interested in acquiring the business) around whom an MBO team can be built (if not, move right to the MBI option). If the answer is 'YES', you need to consider whether you have a suitable team of middle or senior management, which will support the CEO-designate (and put up some of their money). If the answer is 'YES', you need then to address the suitability of the business itself for an MBO. The major areas to consider are whether the business cash flow can service the debt involved in financing the buy-out (which is usually based on borrowed money). Next, you need to establish whether a suitable investor, or lender can be found to finance the buy-out.

Should all these answers be 'YES', you can add an MBO to your shortlist of possible exit options.

Management Buy-ins (MBIs)

Should there be no suitable leader in the business, the next step is to see whether a suitable CEO can be brought in or, alternatively, whether an outside person is interested in undertaking a management buy-out, probably with VC support. Similarly, should you have a suitable internal CEO, but no suitable internal management, you need to consider whether suitable outside management can be brought in to support the CEO. This process is known as a management buy-in (MBI).

If you decide that a suitable leader and/or management from outside are available you would then proceed to examine the business's suitability and the likelihood of venture capital investment support, as you would for an MBO. You do this by moving along the arrow to the left, starting from 'cash flow suitable?'

Should neither an MBO nor an MBI be practical for you, you would now move on to consider the next option, which is Public Listing, or flotation.

Public listing (or flotation)

Although we suggest here that a public listing is considered after the family succession and MBO options, if your business is suitable for a flotation this would, probably, be your first option. A public listing can represent a bonanza to the private business owner, not least because it provides flexibility in disposal, being the first stage in potentially a multi-stage exit plan.

There are two major hurdles in considering your business suitability for listing, namely:

1   Compliance with the relevant Stock Exchange Listing Rules (which usually involve turnover and net asset value tests); and

2   Garnering investment support.

A sponsoring broker would give you preliminary advice on the second issue. If this advice is positive, you should then consider this option very seriously and commission a formal report on the suitability of your business for a public listing. The report would look at such things as the business's financial history and profit forecasts that, if acceptable, would lead to your seeking an underwriter. A positive response from an underwriter would indicate that this exit option is a possibility for your business and should be included on your shortlist.

If a public listing option is not possible for your business, there are still three positive exit options to consider, namely franchising, a trade sale and a merger. (The least positive option of ceasing to trade and an orderly disposal of assets would be your last choice.)

Franchising

To establish whether your business is suitable for franchising you need to ascertain whether the business has a system that can be taught or transferred to third parties who would be prepared to pay for the rights to use it. This means that the system itself would either have to be new, or packaged in a new way; or that the products or services would have to be new, or presented in a new way. Obviously, your business will have to be working well and trading profitably.

The next question to consider is whether you, as the potential franchisor, have the ability to provide back-up services to franchisees, and are also a suitable person to deal with and motivate franchisees on a day-to-day basis. And, of course, suitable potential franchisees must be available in the geographic areas in which you wish to open the franchise businesses.

If all these appear positive, you could ask a franchising expert to provide you with a report on your business's overall suitability for franchising. If this is also positive, franchising could be added to your shortlist for further consideration.

If you feel franchising is not right for your business, you should now move on to the next option, which is a trade sale.

(Note: The choice of an exit option is both a personal one and a business one, and depends on your particular circumstances. You might prefer, for example, to go down the route of a trade sale as your first choice even if a flotation or an MBO are realistic options for your business. Similarly, even if you do have suitable heirs, the value or financial structure of your business may make the family succession option impossible to achieve.

Also, other factors such as your health might mean that a short-term sale – which will, probably, limit you to a trade sale – is the only practical option for you.)

Trade sale (or sale to a third party)

A trade sale is the exit option most utilised by SMEs in the UK. On the face of it, a business needs no particular attributes to be disposed of in this way.

You can now go through the trade sale elimination process. Firstly, is your business solvent, or insolvent? If insolvency is an issue you should get expert legal advice before you try to sell it. Then consider whether it has 'going-concern' status and value, as opposed to a fire sale value only. Next, get some preliminary advice from a business transfer agent (business broker) about the current market for a business of your kind. If all this sounds positive, you can add a trade sale to your shortlist.

Sole trader merger

Businesses merge all the time, but these mergers are often not part of an exit strategy. What we are considering here is the choice of a merger as a deliberate exit strategy for sole traders, or owners of very small businesses. As a sole trader of a small business, in practice your choices of exit options will be limited to a family succession, a trade sale, a sole trader merger, or ceasing to trade.

Looking again at the worksheet, the first point is that, obviously, you need to be a sole trader (or own an overwhelming majority of the business) to qualify for this particular exit option. The next consideration is to decide whether you can find a suitable business with which to merge, and whether the owner of that business is of like mind both in wanting to merge and in general business philosophy. If you think all this is possible it would be worthwhile to undertake some informal research and discussions with potential merger partners to progress the matter before setting out formally to plan your exit through this route.

If, having worked through this and the other options, you decide none is suitable, you now move to the last column on the right and consider ceasing to trade. Here the options are a managed close down (where your company or business is solvent), or liquidation or an administration (if your company is insolvent).

Ceasing to trade

a) Business is solvent

Usually the least preferred exit option for business owners is to cease trading. If your company is solvent you could choose a managed close down with an orderly sale of assets as an exit option. For example, where the business is of the type that loses all value when the current owner leaves or dies (because all the business 'know how' is in the owner's head) a close down might be the only practical way to exit for value.

b) Business is insolvent

Where a company is insolvent, the directors will probably have three choices, namely:

1 *A Company Voluntary Arrangement* Here an insolvency practitioner will attempt to enter into an arrangement with company creditors to accept debt payment over time, or a reduced payment in total, in an attempt to save the company.

2 *Appoint an Administrator* An Administrator's task is to try to dispose of the company as a going concern to realise value for creditors. If there is a surplus after creditors are paid in full, the company's shareholders (or members) will receive a distribution. In most cases of an Administrator being appointed there is no surplus after creditors (and his fees) are paid and, therefore, no distribution to members (i.e. the owners). The usual next step after appointing an Administrator is a winding up.

3 *Appoint a liquidator* The appointment of a liquidator in an insolvent winding up puts the liquidator in charge of the company's affairs and he will act to recover as much as he can for creditors. There is seldom any distribution to shareholders (owners) after creditors have been paid in an insolvent liquidation.

OPTIONS ELIMINATION: REFINING YOUR SHORTLIST

Having been through the steps suggested in the worksheet, you could have decided that only one exit option is available to you. Conversely, you could have more that one option on your short list. Assuming you do have a shortlist, before you make a final decision on the optimum exit option for your business you would need to ask a series of questions, which are listed in Figure 7.3, below.

Refining your shortlist

Ask yourself the following questions:

- Which of the short listed options is likely to result in the maximum price for the business?
- What is the likely impact of taxation on you personally (and any other partners or shareholders in the business) if you adopt this route?
- How long will you need to plan properly for an exit using this option and do you have the time available?
- What is the state of the economy generally and your industry in particular now, and what is it likely to be when you plan to exit?
- Are you personally suited to the option chosen (for example, will you make a good CEO of a public company, or a suitable franchisor of a franchise group?), or is the option largely personality neutral (such as a trade sale)?
- What are the likely costs of proceeding with any particular strategy (or option) compared with the potential increase in the disposal price?
- What will be the impact on your customers, financiers, suppliers and employees?

Figure 7.3. Refining your shortlist.

THE IMPACT OF YOUR DECISION ON THIRD PARTY STAKEHOLDERS

We will now consider the last question in Figure 7.3.

When and how you advise third parties of your intentions to exit your business could be significant, as their reaction could influence the success of the exit, including the eventual price paid. For example, if your senior management finds out at the last minute that you intend to sell and they all resign in protest, you could find that your business is unsaleable. It is important, therefore, to consider in advance how best to handle third parties in your exit plan. The third parties with an interest in your business that we will look at here are the following:

- Family members.
- Minority shareholders.
- Management and employees.
- Trading associates, such as customers, suppliers, bankers and advisers.

FAMILY MEMBERS

We need to distinguish between those businesses in which family members are shareholders and/or employees and those in which they are not directly involved. Taking the latter first, how much and when you tell non-involved family members about your exit plans will always be a matter of personal choice. From an exit planning point of view, it probably has no direct relevance.

Where you have family shareholders and employees in your business, how much and when you involve them in your exit plans could be vital. Broadly speaking, there will be two different exit scenarios here, firstly where the exit is through a family succession and, secondly, where the exit is through some other method.

A family succession

You could have two types of family shareholders in your business, namely, the heirs (to whom you plan to leave the business) and the non-heirs. The heirs should know all about your plans as they will (I hope!) have been closely involved in the timing of their takeover, as well as being trained and groomed over the past several years.

The non-heirs are the more difficult group to handle. Firstly, it is probably a good idea to canvass non-heirs for their views of your succession plan in general and your choice of heirs in particular. Depending on the percentage of shares held by non-heirs and the details of your shareholders' agreement, it might be necessary not only to have their opinion and support, but also to have their formal agreement to any succession plans you have and, in this case, the sooner you advise them of your plans the better. Also, non-heirs might be key employees in the business and crucial to the continued success of the business after transfer.

An exit through other means

Where you plan to dispose of a family business through a method other than a family succession (for example, through a trade sale), from a commercial standpoint family member shareholders and employees would require the same sort of thought as minority shareholders and employees in a non-family company. How you should involve minority shareholders is considered below. However, from a personal point of view you will probably believe that family stakeholders require to be advised of your plans earlier (and perhaps with more detail) than non-family stakeholders.

Minority shareholders

The question we are looking at here is how much and when you involve minority shareholders (in non-family companies) in your exit plans. In all companies, the first consideration is your shareholders' agreement. Where you have one, it should deal with the question of whether minorities are compelled to sell their shares when the majority owner wishes to and, if so, it will guide you in deciding how much and how early you need to involve minorities with your exit plans. Of course, what you *need* to do is not necessarily what you feel you *should* do and it could be a matter of personal preference when you tell minority shareholders of your exit plans.

Where you do not have a shareholders' agreement, the position is completely different. If your plans are to sell the whole company, it is now not a question of merely advising the minorities of your intention to sell: you will need to get their agreement that they will sell their shares. In these circumstances, you need to involve minorities as early as possible in your plans and do one of two things, either get their acknowledgement in writing that they will sell their shares when you wish to sell yours (and on the same terms), or enter into a full shareholders' agreement that compels them to do so.

Employees

The question of when to advise employees that you plan to exit is an extremely difficult one to answer, probably because the relationship between the owner and employees is different in each business and employees themselves are different from business to business. You have two conflicting issues here, namely:

- If you advise employees in advance that you intend to sell out, you are likely to unsettle them and could lose some of your key staff.
- If you do not advise employees of your exit until the last minute, you run the risk of fermenting discontent, which could also result in key staff members walking out!

Also, there is the overriding question of the necessity of retaining confidentiality about your plans so as to ensure competitors do not take advantage of you in the delicate period of finalising your exit.

A good example of the problem in divulging your exit intentions to employees is the following story told to me by an owner of a small business.

'I have sold two businesses in my life,' he said.

'In the first, I was inexperienced and did not tell my employees that I had received an offer from a competitor until the sale agreement had been finalised. As it happened, I lost my sales manager (who had excellent relationships with my biggest customers) and the sale nearly fell through as a result.

'In my second business (which was IT-based) I thought I would not make the same mistake again and when I started to plan to sell I advised my IT manager and other key employees of my decision. When I was close to finalising negotiations for a sale, my IT manager (the most important employee of all) told me he was leaving! It took me 12 months to replace him, during which time the sale was put on hold, turnover dropped and the eventual purchase price was reduced. You can't win.'

So, what do you do? The key to this dilemma lies, I believe, in exploring ways of locking in key employees to your business, thus making it more advantageous for them to stay in the business than to leave it. I discuss this issue in more detail in the next chapter.

Human beings are usually averse to change and if there is no good reason to leave employment, most will stay. However, even if you have introduced effective incentives to stay in your business you still need to consider carefully the best time to advise employees of your exit plans. Some owners I know face this problem up front by advising potential employees at initial interviews of their longer-term exit plans, so that employees are aware that the owner is planning to exit at a certain time and can have no resentment if this happens.

Another approach is to plan employment policy with your exit in mind. In brief, under this approach owners are urged to consider what sort of people they should employ through the life of the business in the light of the exit method and timetable they have planned. I discuss this concept in more detail in Chapter 9 on Tailoring your Business.

TRADING ASSOCIATES

How will your exit affect your customers, suppliers, bankers and advisers, and should you care? Again, there are no hard and fast answers, but in general I believe that outside of special personal relationships, you should not be too bothered about these associated parties. Business is business and change in business ownership is a fact of business life: owners do not in my opinion need to be advising all and sundry.

However, let us consider some special relationships. You may own a business that is the major (or only) customer of a small supplier to whom you feel some sort of responsibility because, perhaps, you have encouraged him to supply only your business. Your likely purchaser could be a 'big brother' in the same industry that is likely to buy his supplies from his current supplier and not your supplier. In this case you might feel it necessary to advise your supplier well in advance of your exit plans.

The introduction of key customers to a new buyer is an integral part of the handover process in the sale of a business. The question is whether the seller should wait until the sale is a done deal, or give some notice to customers of his longer-term plans. The notice (hopefully coupled with a 'best intentions' undertaking to continue with the new owners) could be a condition of purchase and, if so, you will need to deal with this. However, confidentiality could also be the major consideration for the owner and this will need to be weighed in the balance with the advantages (mainly to the potential purchaser) of advising customers of what is happening. (Please note, that the question of the impact on the eventual purchase price if customers are lost after sale is dealt with in some detail in Chapter 12.)

THE METHOD OF EXIT

We have spent some time looking at the question of when to advise stakeholders of your exit plans. This could be influenced by personal sentiment or purchaser pressure. However, just as important could be the method of exit you are considering. In family succession, the need to groom the heir (and, perhaps, get family approval for the plan) necessitates advising all interested parties some considerable time before the transfer itself. Similarly, if you are planning a flotation, there is much to be done that cannot, by its nature, be kept from key employees, so they will need to be advised well in advance. It is, perhaps, in a trade sale (where, with care, the secret can be kept pretty much unknown to anyone other than owners and potential purchasers) that the largest discretion as to when to advise stakeholders exists and the problem of when to advise stakeholders is most acute.

OTHER CONSIDERATIONS

Returning now to choosing a final exit option. The worksheet is a useful way to begin to understand the exit options that could be open to you. We do not pretend that it is the only way, or that it is a substitute for expert advice and an understanding of what works best in your industry. When you have worked through the elimination worksheet and read the following chapters in this book, you will, at least, have a framework to identify the best disposal option for your business with some certainty.

The other considerations that will be important to all owners will be the costs of planning and implementing their chosen exit, the impact of taxation on the particular exit method chosen and whether you have the time and are able to put your business in shape to meet the requirements of the exit option you have chosen.

The costs of exiting your business will vary greatly depending on the route you choose and how much professional assistance you require. For example, should you decide to go down the trade sale route and handle the sale yourself this will be far, far cheaper than floating your company on the Main Board of the London Stock Exchange. But, in reaching this decision the real issue is what are the total net sale proceeds from either route: that is, the net benefit rather than the gross cost. Again, you will have a better idea of this once you have read this book and taken the appropriate advice.

The timing of any business sale is always a difficult issue. It is impossible to be sure of economic cycles and the changes in the financial desirability of industry sectors. Our approach in this book is to advise you to groom your business for disposal through a managed exit strategy with a target date in mind, but also to be prepared to postpone the sale in the case of an economic downturn at the time you plan to sell. Your exit planning should have made big improvements in your company's operations and turnover (and, hence, its profitability), so that you will be reaping current rewards anyway and, hence, be in a good position to wait a while until the market improves, if this is necessary.

The final question is whether you can put your business into the state it needs to be to take advantage of the option you have chosen. For example, will you be able to grow the business (both organically and, if necessary, by acquisition) to reach the minimum size requirement to attract institutional support for a flotation? Or, if you have identified an MBO as your optimum exit route, will you be able to put together a management team that is likely to get the support from VCs that is necessary? In a trade sale, will your business be attractive to the pool of potential buyers you have identified? Positive answers to these questions could rely on whether you have given yourself enough time to plan, or whether you are able to remove the business's impediments to sale, or perhaps it depends on the projected and actual state of the economy with regard to business values in your sector.

THE FINAL CHOICE OF OPTION

You should now have a good idea of the exit options that are realistically available to you and the one that is, probably, your optimum one. The final choice is down to you because, as the business owner, you should be the best person to know the potential of your business and how it can be best presented to advisors and, ultimately, to potential purchasers. Where your own personality is a factor in the success or otherwise of the exit option (such as in a flotation or franchising), you should also be in a good position to know whether you are likely to be up to the task. This knowledge, coupled with a thorough understanding of each option will enable you to reach a measured decision, either on your own, or in collaboration with professional advisors on which option is the one that will maximise your exit outcomes.

SUMMARY

We have now got to the stage of choosing the optimum exit option, which is a convenient place to consider where we have got to with our exit planning so far.

Initially we asked you to establish your business ambitions, or what you wanted from your business. This led you to thinking about your exit. From here we considered some basic issues such as ownership structure, why and when you might exit and the pros and cons of having co-owners. Next we considered Business Continuity Planning and the very important issue of shareholders' agreements. Then we looked at the various exit options available to SMEs, which has brought us to where we are now: how to choose the optimum exit that is best suited to your business.

This brings us to the start of the process of looking at your business's operations, making operational plans and putting the business into shape for exit. This will lead us to identifying and removing impediments to sale and the task of tailoring your business to suit the exit option you have chosen. From here it is a short step to producing a Master Exit Plan, implementing this plan and arranging the disposal itself.

8
Impediments to sale

In this chapter we look at those operational and structural problems in your business that could make it difficult to sell, or which will depress its sale price. The operational issues we call 'impediments to sale', whilst the structural problems could more accurately be called 'barriers to exit'.

First, we explain that not every business is saleable, even if you keep reducing its sale price. We see that this difficulty in selling a business could arise either from negative factors within the business, or from things outside the business that have an impact on its trading.

Next, we consider in more detail what the impediments to sale are and, for convenience, put them into loose structural, operational and miscellaneous categories. We then look at how to identify impediments within a business.

Next, we consider impediments in terms of how long they should take to remove, namely over the long-, medium- and short-term.

Finally, we give you some general ideas on how to remove impediments, including the importance of continuous monitoring of your progress.

INTRODUCTION:
HAVING AN UNSALEABLE BUSINESS

An important fact that might come as a surprise to those unfamiliar with business disposals is that, unlike real property, which will eventually sell, if you reduce the price sufficiently, some businesses will never be sold regardless of their sale price. This is, usually, because the business is a liability. For example, it could be losing money, or be in too much debt; or it could be that potential purchasers think its operations or assets will never earn a profit.

The structural aspects of a business that make it unsaleable could be considered as 'barriers to exit' whilst the operational issues that reduce its attractiveness to buyers I call 'impediments to sale'. Through the exit planning process barriers and impediments to sale should be identified at an early stage and removed (or corrected) over a period of time, hopefully well before the need to sell arises.

As an owner, your objective should be to sell a profitable and vibrant business at the optimum market price. The worst outcome for you will be to try to sell a tired, disorganised business that is shrinking instead of growing steadily, and end up having to close it down. Allowing yourself enough time to remove your business's impediments could be vital if you are to achieve all your exit goals.

DISCOVERING YOUR IMPEDIMENTS TOO LATE

One of the biggest drawbacks of unplanned disposals is that owners often find out about their business's impediments during the process of the disposal itself, usually during due diligence. This can result in a greatly reduced disposal price, or in the sale falling through. Even worse, if you have left an unplanned sale until late in life, it may be too late for you to fix the problems and put the business up for sale again and could result in it being closed down and its assets sold off at fire sale prices.

We will now consider the nature of impediments to sale.

CATEGORISING IMPEDIMENTS

Impediments to sale can be categorised in various ways, two of which are as follows:

1   Types of impediments, being:

   •   Structural barriers to exit, which do not have a direct impact on the operations or profitability of the business.

- Operational impediments, which do have a direct impact on profitability and ultimate business value.
- Miscellaneous impediments (that are not easily classified as either of the above).

2 To rank them by degree of difficulty (and length of time) for their removal, namely long-, medium- and short-term.

First we will consider impediments in the categories of structural, operational and miscellaneous, and then we will look at how long it could take to remove them.

STRUCTURAL IMPEDIMENTS TO SALE, OR BARRIERS TO EXIT

These impediments do not directly affect the trading or profitability of your business, but they do influence either your ability to exit successfully, or the freedom to plan as you would like, or (in the case of lack of taxation planning) the net amount of money you are likely to be able to keep after sale.

OWNERSHIP ARRANGEMENTS: SHAREHOLDERS' AGREEMENTS

Where you have co-owners in a business, the lack of a properly drawn up shareholders' agreement reduces your ability to exit at the time of your choice, because you might need the cooperation of your co-owners to do so. This is a problem that can be prevented by entering into an agreement early in the life or your business, preferably at the time of the share issue.

CHANGES TO THE LAW

Businesses may be based on a demand that springs from legislation, or lack of it. 'Speakeasies' in the United States arose because of prohibition; the home brewing business in Scandinavia is successful because it is legal to brew beer and spirits in Scandinavian homes. Changes in legislation had, and could have, a dramatic effect on both business niches. They could also have a dramatic impact on your business.

Where you are aware that your business will be adversely affected by changes in legislation, you have some stark choices. Either you reinvent your business through developing new products and markets, or you try for a quick sale (which will probably be at a depressed price because your buyer will be aware that he has to fix the problem), or you endure a lingering business death and eventual close down.

INADEQUATE ACCOUNTING PROCEDURES

Poor accounting procedures that produce unreliable or inadequate reports, and/or accounting records in which personal and business expenses are confused, present a business in an unfavourable light. If this problem is not rectified, potential buyers will have no confidence in the performance of the business.

Some owners attempt to rectify this problem by producing 'true' accounts in the year immediately prior to sale, or by providing 'adjusted' accounts to potential buyers. Neither of these solutions is entirely satisfactory. Accurate, professional accounting methods should be introduced at least three years prior to the planned disposal, whilst adjustments to accounts are considered to be acceptable where only legitimate owner-related expenses are removed.

You should also tidy up your balance sheet prior to sale by selling off slow moving or obsolete stock, writing off bad and doubtful debts and selling excess assets. Finally, you should ensure that your statutory accounts are up to date.

LACK OF TAX PLANNING

Although most impediments affect gross business value, just as important are things such as lack of tax planning that will reduce your net sale proceeds. Tax planning for exit is covered in detail in Chapter 10, so I will only make some brief points here.

Three issues are important if you are to receive maximum taper relief from Capital Gains Tax (CGT) when selling shares in a company (or assets in a business) namely:

1   How you own your shares (for example, personally or through a holding company.

2 How long you have owned the shares.

3 Whether your company qualifies as a 'trading company'.

The good news here is that any unfavourable outcomes can be avoided if you allow yourself enough time to structure your affairs correctly before you exit.

(Note: Because taper relief from CGT is available to individuals only, owners of companies will wish to sell their shares, instead of arranging for the company to sell its assets. But, a sale of shares will transfer a company's liabilities as well as its assets to the purchaser, who might not favour this approach. This will put added importance on vendor indemnities and warranties and emphasises the need to ensure that the company is 'clean', with all contingent liabilities settled or removed, including outstanding litigation, before you sell.)

We will now move onto consideration of some of the major operational impediments to sale, before looking at how long it could take to remove impediments in your business.

OPERATIONAL IMPEDIMENTS TO SALE

It has been said that there are as many different impediments to sale as there are different companies. Certainly, in my work I come across different ones (or at least variations of the more common ones) every month. The list of operational impediments below is not meant to be exclusive, but will give you a good idea of what to look out for in your own business

THE BUSINESS IS LOSING MONEY

Generally speaking, it is difficult to sell a loss-making business for anything other than net tangible asset value. Exceptions to this rule can be unprofitable early stage businesses with big profit potential, or a business with valuable intangible assets, or where a purchaser removes the acquired business's overhead costs and adds its sales to his existing operations. Where you are selling a loss-making business, in most cases the best you can hope for is to sell the business as a going-concern and receive marginally more for the assets than they would realise at auction. At worst, the business will fail to attract a buyer and will be broken up, with its assets sold at auction at fire sale prices. (Where the business is insolvent, the directors will probably have to wind it up immediately, with the assets eventually being sold at auction prices.)

GROSS MARGINS ARE TOO LOW

Sometimes a business can be profitable even with very low gross margins, (supermarkets being a good example). But, besides businesses with dominant market share and huge sales, a business with low margins carries a high risk. Investors are particularly wary of businesses with low gross margins relative to their industry sector because of their vulnerability to change, not only in market conditions but also in management and ownership.

Where two businesses are making the same net profit, but one is achieving it from a lower gross sales figure (with a higher gross margin) it will probably command a higher valuation than the other that is achieving its profit from a higher sales figure (and a lower gross margin). As a generalisation, this will be because the one with the lower sales and higher margins will command a higher multiple (such multiple being applied to its profits to arrive at the value) because it is less risky. (This is explained more fully in Appendix 1 on business valuation.)

STATIC, OR DECLINING TURNOVER AND PROFITS

Potential purchasers of a business are usually interested in its future profitability. They are, therefore, attracted to a business whose profit trend is upwards, rather than downwards or static. Most purchasers know that business decline is harder to arrest than many sellers would like them to believe. The lesson here is that you should plan to sell your business when it is on an upward profit curve and not on a downward one.

GOODWILL CANNOT BE TRANSFERRED

There are two issues here.

1   The first is where all the technical skills and/or managerial knowledge necessary to run the business are in the minds of the vendors and there is no remaining management able to assist the buyers, or no time for

the vendors to conduct a proper handover. In other words, 'the owner is the business'. (I have covered this in some detail in Chapter 2.)

2 The other typical loss of goodwill arises when at least one of the former owners plans to go into competition with the business being sold and is not bound by a non-competition provision in the sales contract. This can come about, for example, when the majority of partners decide to sell a business following a partnership dispute in which a dissident partner has been dismissed.

RELIANCE ON A FEW MAJOR CUSTOMERS

Having only a few customers puts the maintainability of current profits (and the business's value) in severe doubt. This is particularly acute when the departing vendor has close relationships with these customers.

It is surprising, but true, that so many businesses will trade for years with only a few customers or clients and make no effort to expand their customer base. These businesses can be very profitable in the hands of the current owners, who are usually unpleasantly surprised by the difficulty of realising a reasonable price on disposal. Technically speaking, the values of these businesses are depressed because the P/E ratio applied to their profits is very low to compensate for the risks involved in maintaining profits.

RELIANCE ON TOO FEW PRODUCTS

Developing new products is usually a long-term task, involving such things as market research design, product development, marketing, etc. Some companies will have existing production facilities and capacity to expand their product range, whilst others will not. Your business's competitive edge might reside in only one or two products (perhaps because of intellectual property or patents pending) and loss of this could be disastrous to the business's value.

KEY CONTRACTS ARE SHORT TERM

Here purchasers will be concerned that contracts will not renew, particularly when the vendor leaves after sale. The problem is similar to having too few customers, above.

Low market share

This is a particular problem with bigger private businesses trying to attract institutional investors or overseas buyers. Research has shown that the businesses with the biggest market share make the biggest profits and if you are in this league, or hoping to move into it, you must increase you share of the market in your industry, or sector, or niche. The time you have given yourself to plan your exit will determine to some extent whether you can achieve an enhanced market share through organic growth or acquisition.

Lack of protection for intellectual property (IP)

Where a business's competitive difference is based on its IP (or where its major activity is the commercialisation of its IP), lack of proper protection of the IP (through a patent or trade mark) could be a major impediment to sale. It would be necessary in these circumstances to secure this protection before trying to exit the business.

Changes in international competition

The competition from low-cost countries (particularly in the Far East) could have a major impact on a business's long-term profitability and ability to survive. Currently, China is emerging as a major threat to UK manufacturing companies, just as India is in the service sector. As with changes to legislation, businesses affected by this type of competition need to move fast to adapt, or see their value disappear.

Lack of agreements with principals, suppliers and employees

When a business's operations are reliant on agency agreements, it is vital that these agreements are current and in writing. Without this a business could be valueless. Business value will be affected to a lesser extent by lack of current agreements with key suppliers and key employees, but it is still important to try to lock in key employees. Note however, a related problem where the potential purchaser might not wish to keep people with whom you have employment agreements. (This problem has been discussed in more detail in Chapter 4.)

VALUE OF ASSETS MORE THAN VALUE OF THE BUSINESS

This problem arises when the total value of the business calculated by conventional methods (such as capitalisation of maintainable earnings or discounted cash flow) is less than the market value of the business's assets, either as a going concern, or as shown on the company's balance sheet. This can arise for several reasons, such as:

1   The business has valuable assets that are not necessary for the production of its income, for example the freehold of commercial premises from which the business operates. Here the simple solution is to sell the property in a separate transaction. With plant and equipment, some work might need to be done to establish which assets are non-essential before they are sold separately.

2   Stock accumulation: where a business has accumulated large stock levels that result in a balance sheet value larger than the business's total market value arrived at through conventional methods of valuation, a sale price based on conventional valuation will, once again, realise less than the business assets are worth. The simple answer could be to try to sell off excess stock separately, although this could have adverse taxation implications depending on how the stock has been treated for tax purposes in previous accounting years.

A HISTORY OF A LARGE TURNOVER OF KEY STAFF

How serious an impediment this is could depend on the type of exit option you choose and the type of buyer that is interested. It will be least serious in a trade sale where the purchaser intends to merge your operation with his own and already employs the staff necessary to undertake all the key functions in your business. But, it could be a fatal impediment where an institution thinking of backing an MBO will be relying entirely on your staff to run the business. Why staff leave any particular business can be a complex issue, but if this is a problem in your business, you should examine all the circumstances involved and try to put permanent solutions in place.

BUSINESS IS TOO DIVERSIFIED: IT CARRIES ON TWO, OR MORE, COMPLETELY DIFFERENT AND INCOMPATIBLE ACTIVITIES

These businesses usually evolve due to the special interests, or skills of the owner, or because of historical reasons. The answer to the problem is usually to separate the businesses and sell the parts separately.

PROFITS ARE DEPRESSED BECAUSE OF EXCESSIVE SPENDING ON NON-ESSENTIAL ITEMS

A business's published profits can be distorted because of excessive owners' drawings. These drawings are usually removed from the 'adjusted' profit statements that are presented to potential purchasers. The impediment I am talking about here is different and arises because current profit is depressed by unusually large expenditure on items not essential for the production of profits in the current accounting period. This expenditure could have been legitimately incurred for the longer-term benefit of the business: an example being an expensive marketing campaign.

The solution to this distortion of current profits is to revert to a normal spending pattern for at least three years before exit, or to amortise this expenditure in the accounts in a way that is more positive for current profits. (Note, if you are a potential purchaser you should be wary of a business that in the accounting period immediately before sale stops spending on things that are essential to maintain profits and, thus, boosts its current profits.)

UNSTABLE MANAGEMENT AND EMPLOYEES

Such people often decide to leave the business when informed of the proposed sale. If you have identified this as a possible problem, the answer is to allow yourself enough time to replace the staff concerned. You should also consider whether the instability arises because you have not provided sufficient incentives for staff to remain. (I have dealt with this in more detail in Chapter 4.)

LACK OF SUITABLY TRAINED MANAGEMENT AND STAFF

This is a different problem to the one where goodwill cannot be transferred due to lack of senior management to carry forward the business knowledge after the owner has left. This problem is at a lower level of management, but impacts on current trading efficiency and profitability. Recognition of the problem and time to fix it are all that is required.

BUSINESS PREMISES

Business premises can be the cause of several problems, such as being located in a remote area that might not suit the purchaser, or having unfavourable lease conditions, or environmental or health and safety problems. Again, these impediments are difficult to fix if left to the last minute. An exit plan that recognises the need to address premises problems and allows sufficient time to do so, should suffice.

OBSOLETE TECHNOLOGY

Depending on the type of business this can be critical; in other cases it can be a serious problem, but one that can be fixed with planning. Alternatively, it could be a fairly minor issue of updating office computer equipment.

ORGANISATIONAL STRUCTURE

This can cover many areas, but of particular interest to buyers is how responsibilities have been allocated among owners, managers and staff. Part of this should be covered in your review of management's ability to assist the new owners, but issues of management to staff ratios, costs and savings could be equally important, as could employee contracts. Other issues, such as the need for branches and how they are managed, should also be reviewed. In brief, buyers wish to purchase a business in which these reviews and the necessary clean ups have been completed prior to sale, rather than after it.

LACK OF A BUSINESS PLAN

This is an impediment to your exit planning for several reasons.

1   Purchasers will think your business is unprofessionally and badly run if it does not have a business plan.

2   Purchasers (who are paying for future profitability) will have no confidence in your profit forecasts unless they are backed up with well-considered projections.

3   Where you wish to raise finance as part of your exit plan (for example, you might want to make an acquisition to beef up your critical mass prior to a public listing, or you might require venture capital financing

for an MBO), not having a professionally prepared business plan will, at best, delay your plans until one is produced.

LACK OF STATUTORY COMPLIANCE IN SUCH AREAS AS ENVIRONMENT AND HEALTH AND SAFETY

This is a very important issue, but one that you can probably remedy within a relatively short time. You should ensure that the business possesses all the appropriate licences and complies with the requisite procedures. It is worthwhile completing a formal audit to ensure complete compliance, as this will probably be required during the due diligence process. Of course, serious site contamination could be a much more serious issue and your audit will bring this to light.

MISCELLANEOUS IMPEDIMENTS TO SALE

THE OWNER'S ATTITUDE AND APPROACH

Here we look at attitudes and circumstances that make it difficult for a vendor to exit his business, or to receive the maximum after-tax proceeds on sale, rather than matters that reduce the intrinsic value of the business itself. The first of these is setting the sale price.

1 Setting an unrealistically high sale price

Owners who have an unrealistic view of the market value of their businesses are, probably, the biggest reason why SMEs are not sold at the first time of asking. Where a business is over-priced and owners will not negotiate its price, the business will usually not sell. Alternatively, if the owner insists on offering the business at an unrealistically high price and is serious about selling it, he will have to reduce the price to achieve a sale. This price reduction is often implemented in stages over a long period, which gives the worst possible signal to potential buyers and puts an unbearable strain on the business, its owners and its key employees. The sensible approach is to ensure that the business is offered for a reasonable price from the outset. By reasonable price I mean one based on a realistic valuation using acceptable valuation methods. The price at which the business is offered need not be the same as the valuation nor the lowest price that you will take, but it must be within a reasonable negotiating distance of your lowest price and should be based on a realistic valuation.

2 Some co-owners not wishing to sell

Although it appears obvious that all owners should agree to sell before the business is offered for sale, and that they should all be working in unison once the business is put on the market, many businesses are put up for disposal where some of the owners are lukewarm, at best, about the idea of selling, or disagree on the selling price. Often, the result is that these owners refuse to negotiate on any offers, or are so difficult in their negotiations that the sale falls through.

Another reason for this problem could be that there is no shareholders' agreement in place that smoothes the way for an exit by establishing that all owners will agree to an exit subject to certain conditions.

3 Owners staying on too long

Where an owner has become tired and disillusioned with his business, trading results can suffer, employees will lack motivation and brand and customer loyalty will be eroded. Staying on too long is an impediment that is difficult to fix once it has occurred: a perfect example of prevention being better than cure. The answer is to plan for an exit in advance to ensure you do not get into this state. If you are already in this position, probably the best you can do is to postpone your disposal whilst you rejuvenate the business either through your own efforts, or through bringing in and training fresh management, or with the help of a business mentor, or a non-executive director.

4 Understanding what buyers want

We discussed earlier the fact that vendors often over price their businesses. Another major difficulty vendors have is that they do not understand what purchasers or investors are looking for in a business. For example:

1   Purchasers are primarily interested in a business's future and not in its past. You may have achieved great things with your business and it may have taken up the best years of your life, but purchasers are only interested in what profits it will make for them in the future.

2   You should try to understand the different motivations of, say, an institutional investor in an MBO and a private buyer in a trade sale. The most obvious one will be that the institutional investor will have a hard-nosed commercial approach to his investment which he wishes to realise through a reasonably quick exit (perhaps by a public listing or a secondary buy-out), whilst the private buyer might be looking at a long-term business that he will work in until he retires and then transfers to an heir.

5 Unwillingness by seller to provide vendor finance

The inability of potential purchasers to raise finance to buy a business is a common problem in SME sales and to achieve their asking price vendors might need to provide vendor finance on terms. But, the consequences of such a loan need to be considered in the light of the vendor's personal financial circumstances.

6 Unwillingness of seller to provide business information to potential buyers

It is not unusual for sellers to be reluctant to provide what they consider to be confidential business information to potential buyers. The problem is particularly acute when the potential buyer is a competitor. The seller wants a commitment before he will provide the information, whilst the buyer will not commit without the information. To counter this problem there needs to be a well thought out, progressive handover of information (depending on the buyer's response and interest) with supporting undertakings of confidentiality. As a seller, you should be aware that you will have to provide virtually all information about your business during the initial negotiating process, whilst you will need to provide *everything* during due diligence. Selling a business is often a painful experience with no guarantee of success, which is why it requires careful planning.

COSMETIC IMPEDIMENTS

Here we are talking about impediments that, although not very serious in themselves, can still have a dramatic impact on the disposal price.

1 Business looks run down, untidy, etc.

In business disposals, like most other areas of life, first impressions can be important. A business's superficial appearance can influence whether a prospective buyer will continue to pursue the opportunity. This impediment is less critical than when the owner himself has run out of steam (resulting in a series of longer-term problems) and can sometimes be solved with an extensive tidying up, or merely by providing new uniforms to factory workers and applying a coat of paint to the factory.

2 Lack of adequate records

This includes such things as records of suppliers, or customers, or sub-contractors that have not been properly maintained. It should be a relatively easy matter to ensure that these are collated and presented in a business-like way. Also, it is necessary to ensure that all intangible and intellectual property has been properly valued and ownership properly documented.

3 Out of date computer equipment

There is a temptation when a business is being sold to leave updating of computer equipment to the purchasers. This could be a mistake as it adds to the look and feel of a run-down business in decline. It could be preferable to update these before sale as part of the cosmetic clean up.

IDENTIFYING IMPEDIMENTS

Identifying impediments is the first step on the road to fixing them. Some impediments and barriers to exit are obvious: for example, you either have an agreement that addresses all the important exit issues between shareholders, or you do not. Operational impediments in your business could become obvious once you have reviewed those listed in this chapter.

A more thorough and scientific approach to identifying operational impediments, however, is to analyse the business's strengths, weaknesses, opportunities and threats (known as a SWOT analysis), as part of the process of producing a business plan (which should be, in turn, part of your exit planning process). Done thoroughly, a SWOT analysis will usually highlight operational impediments to sale.

REMOVING IMPEDIMENTS

All businesses are different in their way and each will have different aspects of their structure or operations that could be improved. A thorough analysis of your business should highlight its impediments to sale and, once they are highlighted, removing them should be, in most cases, a matter of business common sense.

The key to removing most impediments is to allow yourself sufficient time, because some things – such as time qualification for taper relief from CGT – can only be achieved by the passing of time, whereas others by their nature (for example, expanding your customer base or product lines) will need considerable time to fix. Other impediments, although just as damaging to your business's value, will take a shorter time to remove.

Although it is impossible to be too specific about the time that it will take to remove impediments, I will consider some of the major impediments below in terms of how long it should take to remove them. Another way of looking at this is to consider which impediments you should tackle first and how long should you allow for the task.

STRUCTURAL SOLUTIONS

These impediments need to be addressed immediately, not because they will necessarily take the longest to fix, but because they are fundamental barriers to a successful exit. Ideally, you will have addressed them at start-up. If you did not, you should address them now.

Tax efficient ownership of a 'qualifying trading company'

To ensure that you minimise the impact of tax on your disposal proceeds you should get expert tax advice, especially on Capital Gains Tax and Inheritance Tax (see Chapter 10). As you never know when you might be forced to exit your business, you should get this advice immediately.

Lack of a shareholders' or partners' agreement

This could prevent you from disposing of your business when and how you wish. You should obtain expert advice on this immediately as, depending on your relationship with other shareholders, it could take considerable time to put an agreement in place. If you are starting a business with co-owners, you should enter into an agreement when the shares are issued.

Legislative changes

If you are aware of any impending changes to legislation (which might come out of the EU for example), it is vital that you begin to implement the changes to your business immediately to counter any negative impacts.

LONG-TERM SOLUTIONS (MORE THAN FOUR YEARS)

We now move onto operational impediments that could take more than four years to remove, if indeed they can be removed at all. A solution will depend on the severity of the problem in your particular business and whether a remedy is in your hands or not.

Business is losing money

It is vital to tackle this problem immediately, regardless of when you plan to sell. But, losing money is only the effect and you must identify the causes for the losses (which could be any of dozens of reasons) and address those. Because the reasons for losing money are so numerous, it is impossible to suggest a solution to this problem here.

Business with low margins

You will need to analyse your business product by product and division by division to eradicate low gross margin areas, either by working on the cost of goods side or, perhaps, by removing some product lines or activities. This could take considerable time.

Reliance on a few major customers

It will usually be a long-term project for a business to broaden its customer base. Where the total market is confined to a small number of customers this problem cannot be remedied, but even where other customers exist it can be remarkably difficult for an established business to undertake the cultural changes that might be necessary in finding new customers.

Reliance on too few products

A business that relies on too few products for the majority of its sales is highly vulnerable to changes in taste, fashion and attitudes as well as advances in technology, loss of patent protection and/or changes in legislation. As with reliance on too few customers, having too few products puts sales, profitability and associated business value at severe risk.

In family succession an heir who is not ready for ownership

The training of a successor is a very long-term process that can take up to 15 years. If this is your chosen exit option, you should allow yourself this sort of time for the task.

Stock accumulation

Where you have built up large stocks that will make it difficult for you to receive a fair market price for your business, you might need to start selling off stock at least five years prior to your planned sale.

Business premises

If the problem is leased premises that are unfavourably situated or unsuitable in any other way, early action will need to be taken depending on the amount of notice required to quit.

Large turnover of key staff

This can be a complex issue and you need to undertake a broad review. Some of the issues you could consider include the following:

- Examine your pay structure compared with your industry as a whole.
- Do your competitors have employee share acquisition schemes in place?
- How does your in-house pension scheme compare with those of your competitors?
- How good is your working environment?
- Do key employees have a clear understanding of their promotion prospects?
- Do you communicate with key employees about such things as business strategy?

MEDIUM-TERM SOLUTIONS (TWO TO FOUR YEARS)

Typically, the impediments listed below can be rectified within two to four years of your planned disposal. But, generalisations could be dangerous here and the time required to fix the particular problems in your business could take considerably longer. These impediments include the following:

- Business is too diversified.

- Obsolete technology.
- Goodwill cannot be transferred because knowledge and/or skill are all in owner's head.
- Poor accounting methods.
- Depressed profits through expenditure on non-essentials.
- No agreements with principals, suppliers and key employees.
- You have stayed on too long and business is suffering as a result.

If you really wish to get a better price than you are likely to get with an immediate sale, you will need to put another two to three years into the business with a renewed attitude (and, probably new management) to rejuvenate it. This work will include:

- Motivating, or locking in management and key employees who are likely to quit when you sell.
- Training management and key staff to improve productivity.
- Simplifying or cleaning up the management/personnel structure.

SHORT-TERM SOLUTIONS (12 TO 18 MONTHS)

I list below some of the impediments that you should be able to remove within 18 months of your planned exit date.

Lack of a business plan

Preparing a business plan is usually just a matter of allocating the time and getting on with it.

Not all partners/shareholders willing to sell

You should get agreement to sell from all your co-owners, including the price that is being asked and the one that will be accepted, well before you take formal steps to sell. If these issues are covered in a formal way in your shareholders' agreements you should still confirm that you have the shareholders' goodwill and cooperation in the sale process.

Business looks run down, untidy, etc.

Here the remedial action need only be completed immediately before sale, so work backwards from your selling date to decide how long it will take to complete.

Lack of operational records

These need to be shown to potential purchasers and can be completed at any time in the months prior to sale.

Out of date computers, etc.

This can be tackled in the months preceding sale.

There are other things you should do in the year before sale, which do not involve the removal of impediments as such, but are part of preparing your business for the sale process. These include:

Advising and preparing staff for the sale

This is a very important part of your exit planning, as you will want to retain the goodwill of your staff during and after the sale. The timing is also important: you will wish to give reasonable notice to staff of the impending sale, but you do not want to advise them too early in case the sale falls through.

Establishing a realistic price for the business

If you have planned properly for your sale, you will have timed your exit to coincide with achieving a certain value for your business, or to coincide with a timescale. Unrealistic sale prices are a major impediment to the successful and timely disposal of private businesses, so before putting your business on the market you should establish a realistic market value based on sound economic principals. This will give you a reference point to set your asking price. This valuation can be established any time in the year before sale.

Advising suppliers, customers and bankers of your plans

This should be done shortly before the sale is completed.

GENERAL IDEAS ON REMOVING SALE IMPEDIMENTS

Although the programme for removing impediments will be different for each business, it will help if you follow the general guidelines below:

• Start early: all business problems take longer to fix than is first thought.

- Be realistic: can you fix the problems yourself or do you need outside help? (In some cases you might be the reason the problems exist in the first place. If so, are you really the right person to fix them?)
- If you have used advisers to identify the problems, are these advisers the best people to fix the problems?
- Are your current legal and taxation advisers sufficiently expert to advise you on some of the more technical issues? Do you, perhaps, need a second opinion?
- Always keep your goals in mind: the long-term rewards of removing impediments to sale justify a great deal of effort and some expense.

An important part of removing impediments is the continuous review process of your plans that you should undertake. When you have produced an operating business plan, it should contain objectives and 'things to do' to achieve those objectives. Included in your objectives will be the removal of impediments to sale that you have identified (perhaps through your SWOT analysis). The business plan should be reviewed regularly (usually every three to six months) and you should monitor your progress with regard to how far you have been successful in removing the impediments.

The common impediments to sale and barriers to exit in a business are as follows:

a) **Structural issues**
 1 Lack of shareholders' agreement.
 2 Inadequate accounts.
 3 Changes in competitive threats.
 4 Lack of tax planning.

b) **Operational issues**
 1 Business is losing money; inconsistent trading performance.
 2 Gross margins in the business are too low.
 3 Business has low market share.
 4 Goodwill cannot be transferred: owner is the business; lack of management support for incoming owners.
 5 Reliance on too few customers or clients; key contracts are short-term.
 6 Reliance on too few products.

7   Changes to the law.

8   Lack of IP protection.

9   Supplier, agency or other agreements lapsed, or not in writing.

10 History of a large turnover of key staff.

11 Lack of a business plan.

12 Lack of suitably trained staff and management.

13 Lack of suitable employee and management agreements.

14 Obsolete or redundant plant and equipment.

15 Out of date, lapsed and uncommercial agreements with principals, suppliers, etc.

16 Lack of compliance with trading regulations, licences, etc.

17 Too high value of assets compared with total business value.

18 Inadequate private company accounting methods: profits depressed because of personal expenses, cash sales not recorded, statutory accounts not up to date, etc. Profits depressed by non-essential expenses.

19 Non-synergistic business divisions or activities.

20 Business Premises:

  • Lack of compliance with environmental, health and safety and other regulations.

  • Premises are located in a remote or unsuitable area.

  • Lease conditions, which are not compatible with the potential purchaser's needs.

21 Lack of marketing, sales and employee records.

22 Business looks run down and untidy.

c) Personal and general reasons

1   Owners have set an unrealistic sales price.

2   Owners do not understand the needs or motivation of purchasers.

3   Some owners are unwilling, or reluctant to sell (untidy share register, or lack of shareholder agreement).

4   Timing is wrong: economy is depressed, equity values are low, finance is hard to raise.

5   Lack of personal taxation planning.

6   Owner has stayed on too long – business has suffered accordingly: it looks and feels run down.

Figure 8.1. Common impediments to sale.

SUMMARY

So, what can we learn from this chapter?

1 Impediments to sale are those aspects of a business that reduce its attractiveness and value to potential buyers. They can even make a business impossible to sell.

2 Impediments can be categorised into two main groups, being:

- Structural barriers to exit (which could prevent an exit altogether), and

- Operational impediments (what makes a business unattractive to buyers, reduces its value, or makes it difficult to sell).

3 Although there are impediments that are common to many small businesses, each business owner needs to analyse his own business to identify those which will hamper his exit plans: this can be done through a SWOT analysis when you are producing a business plan.

4 You should start early on the task of removing impediments and you should monitor your progress on a continuous and frequent basis.

9

Tailoring your business to fit your exit options

To recap, so far in this book I have taken you through the conventional steps of planning for your exit. These steps have been:

- Setting your personal objectives.

- Getting your business structure right.

- Establishing a realistic exit timetable.

- Choosing the optimum exit option.

- Identifying and removing impediments to sale (which is part of the process of grooming your business in readiness for disposal).

In this chapter I wish to examine what I consider to be the ideal way to plan for your exit, namely that you should develop and grow your business from start-up to fit your chosen exit option. In other words, you should 'tailor' your business from its beginning with your exit option and your potential purchasers firmly in mind. In doing this, you should remember that exit planning is not an isolated event: it is a long-term process.

This chapter will cover the following:

- The pre-requisites of a business for it to be suited to a particular type of exit option.

- The different types of buyers and investors who are interested in acquiring businesses.

- What these different buyers and investors could be looking for in a business.

- How you should tailor your business to fit both the exit option you have chosen and what you believe buyers/investors are looking for.

To illustrate these points, we will use examples of exit through a trade sale, an MBO and a family succession.

For those of you already in a business who have not begun tailoring your business to fit your exit, all is not lost. By starting your exit planning now you can still be ahead of most of your competitors!

INTRODUCTION

To tailor your business for exit you need to take four main steps, namely:

- **Step 1**: Establish as early as possible in the life of your business what your optimum exit option is likely to be.
- **Step 2**: Ask yourself: what kind of business will I need to develop to ensure I can successfully exit through my chosen route? (Another way of looking at this is to ask: who are my potential purchasers/investors and what are they looking for in the type of exit I have chosen?)
- **Step 3**: Ask yourself: in what ways does my business shape up to these criteria or, alternatively, what are its shortcomings, or likely impediments to sale?
- **Step 4**: Once you have established these criteria, prepare and execute a strategy to 'tailor' your business to fit your chosen exit path.

THE OPTIMUM EXIT OPTION

CHOOSING THE OPTION

In Chapter 7 I considered the ways in which you could choose the exit option most suitable to you and your business. You may wish to revisit this chapter to remind yourself of its contents. You will recall that having examined your personal situation (which included your personal preferences and needs), we looked at an elimination worksheet, which helped you ask simple questions about your business (its size, management, growth potential, etc.) that assisted in establishing what sort of exits were possible. Then we suggested you consider other things, such as taxation and the time available for exit planning, before you made your final choice of one (or possibly two) exit options. Finally, we suggested that, if you were still unsure, you might need professional help with the final decision.

The material covering exit options in Chapter 7 applies largely to established businesses. I wish, however, to say a bit more for those of you who have just begun a new business, or are thinking of starting one.

ESTABLISHING THE OPTIMUM EXIT OPTION FROM START-UP

Where you have just started up a business, some of the material in Chapter 7 might seem inappropriate. In particular, you might (quite reasonably) think that your business is not developed enough for you to follow the elimination worksheet and chose an exit option.

If you have just started a business, you could take a slightly different approach, as follows:

• Follow the steps in Chapter 1 to establish your personal goals and business objectives.
• This will enable you to establish the type of business you are setting up.
• Which will, in turn, assist you in establishing the exit route that will be suitable for your business.

Although the answers to the questions in Chapter 1 will go a long way to establishing how you believe you should exit, your business circumstances could change and so could your exit options. But keeping in mind the necessity of tailoring your business for exit, as you build your business, should help you to be prepared and flexible when the time for exit (and, perhaps, more detailed exit preparation) comes round.

One of my clients summed up the approach I am talking about when he said:

'From the very beginning of our business we managed it as if we were a public company, because we wanted to have the flexibility of going public if the opportunity arose.'

Once you have established your optimum (or likely) exit option, the next step is to consider what sort of business you should be developing to fit this exit.

WHAT SORT OF BUSINESS SHOULD I DEVELOP?

This question is best approached in two parts, namely:

a) What sort of business do I need to develop if it is to qualify for the exit option I have chosen?

And the related question of:

b) What will potential purchasers or investors be looking for in my business when I dispose of it through my chosen exit route? (To answer this question you need to consider the type of purchasers or investors that you are aiming at.)

In Chapter 6 I gave you an overview of the exit options available to private businesses. In this chapter to illustrate what I mean by developing (or tailoring) your business for exit, I will examine the pre-requisites of a business for it to qualify for the exit routes most commonly adopted by SMEs in the UK, namely a trade sale, a management buy-out and a family succession.

A TRADE SALE

DOES MY BUSINESS QUALIFY?

In theory, all types of businesses qualify for exit through a trade sale, in so far as a trade sale does not normally require you to achieve benchmarks of size, quality of management, ability and background of owners, number of branches, and so on. To achieve a successful trade sale is more a question of grooming the business to increase its value and to ensure its obvious impediments to sale have been removed and to choose a time for exit that is propitious as far as the general economy and your particular sector are concerned. But, as a useful guide, please refer to Figure 9.1, below, which is a checklist of the main things you need to do to ensure your business is prepared for a trade sale in most circumstances and whoever the buyers might be.

'Tailoring' for a successful trade sale

For a successful trade sale you need to have developed your business to ensure that:

1 You have a tax effective ownership structure and, where applicable, arrangements with co-owners on transfer of shares.

2 Profits show a year-on year increase for at least three years prior to sale (rather than being flat or declining).

3 The business's trading accounts comply with acceptable accounting standards and show the true position of the company.

4 The business complies with health and safety, employment, environmental and other legislation.

5 You have removed all the business's obvious impediments to sale – see Chapter 8.

6 You have suitable senior, or middle management in place and locked in.

7 The business has a diverse customer base.

8 The business has current contracts with all customers, staff, key management and employees.

9 The business has effective financial controls and operating systems.

10 The business has a professionally produced business plan and realistic growth strategy.

11 The business appears vibrant and growing, rather than tired and declining.

Figure 9.1. 'Tailoring' for a successful trade sale.

WHO ARE YOUR POTENTIAL BUYERS IN A TRADE SALE?

You will now need to decide what type of buyer you are targeting and what these buyers are likely to be looking for in your business. It will help if we establish some basic concepts and definitions about buyers in trade sales.

1 Trade sale buyers are usually divided into two groups, called

'financial' and 'strategic' buyers. Financial buyers consist of owner/managers and those wishing to operate the business on their own. Strategic buyers are institutional and other buyers who look to take over, or merge the target business within their own operations. The strategic buyer classification also applies to what are known as 'industrial partners', or a 'big brother' from your own industry.

2   Disposals though a trade sale can be for all, or a majority, or minority part of a business. Minority sales in the UK are often to venture capitalists (known as VCs), or private investors (who are often known as 'Business Angels'). Majority sales could be to strategic buyers or industrial partners.

3   You should also be aware that a strategic investor (who could be a public company) is likely to take a very long-term view of its purchase, whilst the financial purchaser could have a short-term exit strategy.

4   It is usual for VCs and Business Angels to take minority stakes in businesses, and rely entirely on senior management to run the business. Here your approach might be to partly exit the business as step one in a two-staged exit plan. Your first step could be to sell a minority interest to investors and remain in the business as CEO for an agreed period. Step two could be to sell the balance of the equity to the investors after you have groomed a senior manager for the CEO role. Alternatively, the investors will have their own exit strategy, which could be for a sale of the whole business through a flotation, or through a secondary buy-out (that is, a sale to another VC), thus ensuring that you fully exit the business at this stage.

WHAT ARE BUYERS LOOKING FOR?

General

Generally, a trade sale buyer will be looking either for:

- a business from which to earn a living (and make a capital gain); or
- an investment from which to earn a return, either on its own or to add to an existing operation.

Those who are primarily looking to make a living from the stand-alone business are usually considered to be financial buyers, whilst the investors with wider aims are usually considered to be strategic buyers.

From the seller's point of view the key issue is to discover what particular aspects of your business will assist buyers to achieve their aims. For example, is it your particular products that a strategic buyer wishes to add to his existing business that will make your business attractive to him, or your customer base, or the geographic area in which you operate?

Financial buyers

Financial purchasers are usually individuals who wish to run the business full-time as owner/operators; or investors who will not, necessarily, wish to put all their time into managing the business. In either case, they will usually require that key senior management remain in the business after transition. Where you believe that you are likely to sell to a financial buyer, it is important therefore that you:

- ensure that you have competent senior management in your business well before you exit; and
- put in place retention strategy procedures (for example, a bonus or profit sharing scheme) that improve the likelihood that these managers will stay in the business after transfer.

Also, many individual financial buyers are not very sophisticated when it comes to accounting, so for these buyers your accounts should be presented in a straightforward manner.

Strategic buyers

Here your buyers could be competitors from your industry sector, larger institutions, or VCs. These buyers could be looking at your business not as a stand-alone entity, but one that has attractive synergies with (or add-ons to) their existing business. These synergies or add-ons could come from such things as gaining access to your customers, contracts or geographic market; adding your products to their own; taking over your management and staff (see below); or merging your overheads with theirs.

Where your target buyer is a larger institution, you could have a dilemma with regard to what you should do about senior management. In some cases, the institution will wish to acquire sales turnover only and will strip away most of the overhead of the target business, including most of the staff. In this case, having senior management in your business will be an impediment to sale, because the purchasers will not wish to take them over and incur the cost of redundancies.

On the other hand, some institutions might wish to keep your business as a stand-alone entity, thus relying on its senior management to keep it operating efficiently. In this case, not having senior management could be an impediment to sale!

The only answer to this is to try to find out in advance who, specifically, your buyers might be. In many closely-knit industries this is not too difficult. For example, if you have an optician's business you might be aware that the most likely purchasers of your business are franchise groups who are looking for operations like yours with a view to converting them into franchisees. In this case, it is obviously worth your while to establish in detail what these groups are looking for in target businesses (both with regard to management structure and, perhaps, gross margin levels) and then to tailor your business specifically with these buyers in mind.

Besides senior management considerations, it is helpful for you to understand what VCs and Business Angels expect by way of return on their investment. VCs will be looking for a high return and a likely exit in five to seven years. They are attracted to businesses that have a chance of going public, or being on-sold at a significant profit. (You need to bear in mind, however, that very few private businesses have a realistic chance of taking the flotation route.)

Business Angels are a mixed bag of individuals. Some of them take a professional investment approach by seeking high returns through a three to five year exit (and will keep at arm's length from your business in the meantime). Others will be quite happy to be involved in the business in a non-executive capacity with no particular rate of return, or exit time frame in mind: these people might be, simply, looking for something exciting to do!

A MANAGEMENT BUY-OUT (MBO)

DOES MY BUSINESS QUALIFY?

In an MBO (unlike in a trade sale) both the company and its management (who will make up all, or some of the buyers) usually need to comply with certain prerequisites to qualify. This is explained more fully below. But first, we will look at the various types of MBOs.

You will recall from Chapter 6 that management buy-outs can be in four basic versions, namely:

*   A traditional MBO.
*   A management buy-in (or MBI).
*   Sale of 100% of the equity to management.
*   An employee buy-out (or EPO).

It is not always easy to be sure in advance whether your buy-out will be a traditional MBO or an MBI, or whether the purchasers will be your managers and/or employees with or without any institutional partners. But, before you consider this aspect in detail, it is probably a good idea to remind yourself of the three important general questions that need to be answered in the affirmative before you can seriously consider an MBO and, therefore, before you tailor your business for this exit. These are:

1   Does the business have suitable management?

2   Do historical financial reports and cash flow projections show that the business has adequate maintainable cash flows to service the requisite borrowings?

3   Does the business have strong growth prospects?

The importance of these characteristics will become clearer as we consider each type of MBO more closely. But first, consider Figure 9.2 below which summarises the qualifications of a business for a traditional MBO.

Qualification for a traditional MBO

When tailoring your business for a traditional MBO you should bear the following pre-requisites in mind:

1   Businesses in most industries qualify for MBOs.
2   There is no upper limit, in theory, to the size of the deal, but most VCs are unlikely to be interested in deals smaller than £2 million, although VC Trusts will invest in deals as small as £500 000.
3   The business itself should have the following pre-requisites:
   a) It should be able to generate consistent positive cash flows sufficient to service the borrowings necessary in what will be a leveraged transaction. Proof of this ability should be evidenced in recent performance as well as being based on realistic cash flow and profit projections.
   b) Ideally, the business should be in a position to borrow heavily against its own assets. The equity injection from VCs and management is usually relatively small and the business will need to borrow to complete the purchase. (It should be noted that there are certain legal constraints on a company using its own assets as security to purchase its shares, and owners and managers would need to get expert legal advice in this area.)
   c) Where a business has limited capacity to borrow in the form of hard security, the strength of the cash flows and the bank's willingness to lend against them will become paramount.
   d) The business should be well established and, ideally, have a strong position in its market.
   e) Current investment fashion can affect investment decisions. Traditionally, investors have preferred high or medium technology businesses because they are perceived to have higher growth potential.
   f) The business should have strong growth prospects. This is especially important to VC investors.
   g) The business should have a multi-skilled management team, led by a competent leader or CEO, which has a strong desire to acquire the business. The CEO must have the respect and support of the management team.
4   It is essential that the management team has prepared a current, professionally drawn up, well-reasoned and realistic five-year business plan for the business it hopes to purchase, if it is to attract support from banks and interest from VCs. Most management teams will seek assistance with the production of the plan from their accountants, or from a corporate finance specialist.

Figure 9.2. Qualification for a traditional MBO.

A MANAGEMENT BUY-IN (MBI)

All of the characteristics of a traditional MBO listed in Figure 9.2 above, apply to a company that is seeking to exit through an MBI with one very important exception: where there is no one suitable for the role of CEO, or other key management function within the business, the investors will insist that outside expertise be brought in to cover this deficiency before they will give the buy-out their financial support.

When planning for a management buy-out you should always be alert to possible management shortcomings. Where you recognise that your management is weak in some area, you will need to put someone else in place. If this is not possible, you need to accept that the VC investors will insist on bringing in a recognised industry expert as a part of the team. This could completely change the dynamics of the buy-out team and your ability to negotiate the most favourable deal.

SALE OF 100% TO EMPLOYEES

There are two possibilities here, either management will attempt to acquire all the equity with their own money or, more likely, with traditional bank finance; or if the buy-out is an EPO, a specialist EPO financier will provide both equity and debt support.

To prepare your company for this type of buy-out you need to be aware of the following:

1   Where the management is buying your business without any borrowings, the central issue is whether the business is attractive enough for them to offer you your asking price. In these circumstances, the transaction is more like a trade sale than a management buy-out.

2   Where the management is putting up some of the purchase price only and is borrowing the rest, the business will still need to comply with the traditional MBO under points 3 and 4 in Figure 9.2, because the business assets will be security for the borrowings. This is very important because, from my experience, most management/employee buy-outs that fail do so because they are unable to acquire the finance they need.

WHAT ARE BUYERS/INVESTORS LOOKING FOR?

MBO

There are no hard and fast rules to determine which businesses VCs and banks will support in a traditional MBO. Investment fashions are subject to change, whilst each financial institution will have its own particular investment policy. However, as a generalisation, VCs will consider a business that has the following attributes:

- A reasonable asking price arrived at through an acceptable valuation method.
- High growth potential, supported by a professionally produced business plan and a trading record that supports the financial projections.
- In a high tech sector, such as medical and related industries.
- Acceptable CEO supported by suitably competent and entrepreneurial management that is prepared to invest some of its own money in the buy-out.
- The ability to borrow against its own assets.
- Feasible exit strategy, preferably through a flotation or a secondary sale, within five to seven years.

MBI

VCs will look for the same aspects in a business that is being considered for an MBI as they will in an MBO. The only difference is that where the CEO or management is not deemed to be worthy of their support they will need to bring in someone (usually at CEO level) whom they are prepared to support and whom they are confident will achieve the business targets that have been set.

Management/Employees acquiring 100% of the equity

It is difficult to generalise about what type of business the management and employees will be looking for in this type of buy-out, as the motivation for launching buy-outs will vary widely. However, it is safe to assume that management will be looking for all or most of the following before they will go ahead with the transaction:

- Business must have sufficient growth potential for management to believe that buying it is a better option than being employed elsewhere.

- The business owner must set a reasonable sale price and, where necessary, be prepared to offer terms of purchase.
- The business must be able to support the purchase borrowings.
- The management team must believe they can improve the business because of their expertise. Most management teams believe they can do a better job than the current owner!
- A realistic, profitable exit strategy that will justify their risk and hard work.

Where a specialist EPO financier is assisting an employee buy-out, it will look for similar attributes in a business as are necessary for a traditional MBO.

Can they afford the property?

Consider two facts:

1 A significant part of the value of many businesses is the real property from which they operate, being factory, warehouse or office premises.
2 The vast majority of management or employee buy-outs are funded by debt, as employees traditionally do not have large amounts of spare capital.

Obviously, purchasing real property with the business can be a problem for an MBO team, so if you plan for your business to be bought by your management or employees you need to consider whether it is feasible to include in the sale the real property from which the business operates. On the one hand, including the property will push up the sale price but, on the other, excluding it will reduce the hard assets available as security to support the borrowings.

If the company that owns the business also owns the property (as apposed to it being owned by another company or the owner privately) a sale of shares will automatically mean the property will be included in the sale. If you own the property in your own name, you can exclude it from the sale and rent it to the new business. There are also capital tax advantages in owning the property as an individual, rather than through a company.

Once you have decided that an MBO or an EPO is the optimum exit option you should review the ownership of any business properties and allow yourself time to adjust their ownership if necessary, subject to expert advice.

A FAMILY SUCCESSION

A family succession is different from all other exit options in so far as the emphasis is often not on maximising the owner's exit price, but rather on ensuring that the business continues successfully under the ownership of the successor. Consequently, the tailoring (or grooming) is concentrated on the successor, rather than on the business. This alters the perspective of the business's suitability for the exit option chosen and the notion of what purchasers are looking for. This will become clearer from what follows below.

DOES MY BUSINESS QUALIFY FOR A FAMILY SUCCESSION?

Generally speaking, most types of businesses qualify for a family succession. However, if the successor is required to borrow money against the business's assets to acquire the business, the business will need to be able to support the borrowings and the successor will need to have a professionally produced business plan demonstrating this ability. As a guideline in these circumstances, the pre-requisites in points 3 a), b), c) and 4 in Figure 9.2 above, will apply.

WHAT ARE POTENTIAL BUYERS LOOKING FOR?

As I have said, the emphasis in family successions is usually more on the suitability of the heir than the suitability of the business, so this question has to be changed to: 'What are we looking for in the successor?' This will influence the choice of successor and the way he or she should be groomed for the take over.

We will now look at the steps necessary for grooming (or tailoring) the heir for taking over the business.

Choosing your heir

The first step in any family succession plan is to choose the appropriate heir for the business. Where there is only one heir, it is necessary to decide whether he or she wishes to, and is capable of, taking over the business. If there is more than one suitable candidate, it is necessary to decide which one will be chosen. The factors to consider include business aptitude and management potential. Potential is more important than experience, because you can groom your heir for the role as owner/manager over an extended period.

In theory, the steps involved and the logic employed in choosing the appropriate heir should be similar to those involved in choosing the best CEO for the business, or the lead manager in a management buy-out: that is, the heir you choose should be the one most capable of running the business successfully when you leave. In practice, however, the choice may be made for various personal and family related reasons, rather than on solid business-based grounds.

Where there is only one heir (or only one heir who is interested in taking over the business), obviously it might still be a mistake, on purely business grounds, to hand over the business to that heir. But, if this is to be the case, your task is to make the best of a dubious decision and to prepare this person as best you can for the role of running the business.

Common mistakes in choosing an heir

Where there is a choice of more than one heir to take over the business, mistakes (viewed from a purely business point of view) are still made. The usual reasons why these mistakes are made can be seen in Figure 9.3, below.

- The chosen heir is considered to be the one with the most need, rather than the one with the most ability.
- Because the first choice candidate is not willing to take over the business, a second and less suitable candidate is chosen.
- The heir is the family favourite (for personal rather than business reasons).
- Because the business owner has two children, both are chosen, although one might be totally unsuitable.
- Two heirs are given a 50:50 shareholding and equal management status, leading to conflict, or even deadlock.
- The best choice is female, but is considered unsuitable because of her sex and a less able male heir is chosen instead.

- The chosen heir is the dominant personality amongst the children, but is not the best candidate from a purely business point of view.

Figure 9.3. Common mistakes in choosing an heir.

In short, the choice of an heir is often a subjective one based on family sentiment and/or family values rather than on business criteria. But, it is better to make a less than perfect choice than to make no choice at all and leave it to your heirs to sort it out themselves when you have passed on.

Preparing your heir for succession

Probably the most important aspect of a family succession is to prepare (or groom) your heir for the task of owner/manager of the business. It is important that the succession timetable is framed not only to suit the retiring owner, but also to enable the heir to go through all stages of preparation or training at a pace that is suitable for him or her. A period of hands-on management and simulated ownership could be necessary before the handover is completed.

From Chapter 6, you will have seen that it is usual to divide the heir's training into *Learning, Doing, Managing, Leading* and *Outside experience*. This training should begin as soon as the heir joins the business or, at least, as soon as the decision to hand over the business to the heir has been made. We will consider each of these steps in turn.

Learning An involvement with all aspects of the business (even if only superficial) should start soon after the heir first joins the business. This is vital for the heir's future development. You should involve the heir in as many functions of the business as possible.

Doing The heir should be given freedom to partake in all business functions. If the heir has any obvious weaknesses, these should be worked on, or you should ensure that these can be covered, or compensated for in the heir's eventual management team. Undergoing this objective assessment of the heir's weaknesses is a valuable contribution to his or her future management success.

Managing The heir's operational management skills can be gradually developed, so that by handover he or she should have had sufficient experience to manage all aspects of the business.

Leading Besides learning how to manage, the heir needs experience in leading other managers and running the business. Although leadership is largely an inherent skill, team leadership and decision-making can be taught to most competent managers. By the time of the handover, the heir should be capable of making the strategic decisions necessary to be an owner/manager.

Outside experience It is essential that heirs have some business experience outside the family business. Preferably, this should be early in their careers and before training for the ownership process has begun. If this has not happened, time must be set aside (a minimum of two years) for heirs to gain this experience. This will be of great personal benefit to the heir, and ensure greater credibility and respect in the eyes of the management and employees of the business when he or she returns.

SOME FURTHER IDEAS ON TAILORING YOUR BUSINESS TO FIT YOUR EXIT

So far we have considered some ideas for tailoring a business to suit the specific exit options of a trade sale, an MBO and a family succession. In Figure 9.4, below we consider some general rules (which may seem obvious to some readers) for tailoring your business with your exit timetable and exit option in mind.

1   The planned time of your exit should influence every one of your strategic decisions.

2   You can preclude the possibility of exiting by a profitable exit route by some action whose consequences you do not necessarily foresee. For example, you can make it very difficult to go public if you have issued excess share options to senior management.

3   Never make an investment that pays off in 10 years if you plan to exit in five.

4   When you are hiring people think of your proposed exit route. For example, will they be possible buyers in an employee buy-out?

5   When hiring, consider your proposed exit timetable. For example, is it fair to employ a young career-minded person who will probably be dismissed when you fulfil your plan to sell to a competitor in three years' time?

> **6** Keep key management and staff apprised of your plans: if they wish to leave it is better that they do so earlier (when you have time to do something about it), than later (when you have not).

Figure 9.4. General rules for tailoring your business for exit.

SUMMARY

Tailoring a business from start-up is the ideal way to plan for exit. The important point to remember for start-up businesses is that you need to be flexible in your planning approach. You need to be aware that a business will change as it grows and its exit opportunities might change as it develops. However, if you develop your business with your exit always in mind you will be well placed to take advantages of any changes and will be ahead of the game when it comes to fine-tuning your exit plans as you get nearer to your actual exit date.

For those businesses that are already operating, the opportunity to tailor your business from start-up has, strictly speaking, passed. However, you should begin your exit planning immediately (as if you had just started up), because the sooner you get on board the exit train, the more prepared you will be for any unforeseen circumstances that could occur. The general principles of tailoring a business explained in this chapter are just as relevant for mature business as they are for a start-up businesses.

Finally, remember what was said earlier in this book: 'The best time to start planning your exit is from start-up. The next best time is now!'

10

The impact of taxation

The aim of this chapter is to alert you to the issues you should be aware of and the sorts of questions you should be asking your taxation advisers early in the exit planning process. The chapter includes the following material:

- An overview of the taxes that are important in the disposal of a business.

- The principles of Capital Gains Tax and Inheritance Tax.

- The relevance of time and timing in reducing tax liabilities, which reinforces the need to seek competent tax advice well in advance of your planned disposal.

- Checklists to help you ask your tax advisor the right tax planning questions.

DISCLAIMER

The taxation law that applies to the disposal of business assets is extremely complex and is changing all the time and a book of this kind can provide only a basic overview of the issues involved. You should note carefully the following points:

- The material in this chapter does not purport to provide taxation, accounting, and financial or legal advice.
- Owners planning to dispose of their businesses should obtain independent legal, accounting and taxation advice early in the planning process.
- The circumstances of each business disposal are different. You cannot rely on the fact that the general principle will, necessarily,

apply to you and your business. Consequently, independent taxation advice on your particular situation is always necessary.

- If you dispose of your business without early taxation planning you might not be able to take full advantage of the various allowances and reliefs available to you, because many of them are complex and to comply requires a careful arrangement of your affairs well before the actual time of disposal.
- In all circumstances (and particularly if you are retiring) you should consider the effects of tax on your overall business and personal financial position; that is, you must take an integrated approach to your financial and business affairs.
- The Inland Revenue publishes numerous leaflets and booklets on all aspects of taxation. Most of these are available without charge from your nearest Inland Revenue office and on the internet at: *www.inlandrevenue.gov.uk.*

WHAT TAXES ARE IMPORTANT IN EXIT PLANNING?

Income tax, corporation tax, Inheritance Tax and Capital Gains Tax will all have a bearing on your exit planning. For most exit strategies, Capital Gains Tax (CGT) is likely to be the most important, as the proceeds of disposal are the resources that you most need to protect. However, for those owners considering a disposal through a family succession plan, Inheritance Tax (IHT) could be equally important.

Income and corporation taxes will be relevant to the proceeds of the sale of trading assets in the accounting year in which you sell. Income tax, corporation tax and CGT will also be very important in the period leading up to disposal. For example, when you are considering how to allocate the potential trading surpluses in your business between income drawings and capital reinvestment, the interplay of income and corporation taxes and Capital Gains Tax will be a key issue.

CAPITAL GAINS TAX (CGT)

GENERAL PRINCIPLES OF CGT

CGT, like most taxation subjects, is fairly technical and it will help to explain some of the definitions used in the legislation.

- As a general rule, CGT applies to the gain made on the sale of an asset owned and disposed of by the same person or entity. Gain is the difference between the cost of acquiring the asset and the amount received on disposal of it. The amount received when you sell an asset is called the 'disposal proceeds'.
- Where you dispose of an asset at less than cost, you incur a capital loss. Allowable capital losses can be offset against capital gains, but not usually against income profits.
- CGT is payable on the 'taxable amount', which is an amount arrived at after calculating the 'total chargeable gain' and deducting from it various losses, allowances, costs, exempt amounts and 'reliefs'.
- The 'annual exempt amount' is the fixed amount of taxable gain you are allowed in any year and is deducted from the total chargeable gain before CGT is payable. The annual exempt amount for 2004/2005 is £8200.

The order in which these allowances and reliefs are applied is important and we will examine these issues in more detail below.

- Any form of property may be an asset for CGT purposes, including stocks and shares, machinery, land and buildings and all business assets, including goodwill. Certain assets are exempt by the Inland Revenue (IR) from CGT, including private motor cars; proceeds from ISAs, PEPs, TESSAs and UK Government stocks; and betting and lottery winnings. The gain on sale of your private home is also usually exempt from CGT.
- Disposal proceeds will, usually, be in the form of cash, whose amount (or value) is obvious. But where proceeds are not in cash, the concept of 'value' is used. Where the disposal is 'not at arm's length' (that is, not between independent parties for fair value), 'market value' is estimated and used as the basis for calculating disposal proceeds.

ALLOWANCES AND DEDUCTIONS

Losses

You are allowed capital losses from the current tax year, or they can be carried forward from previous tax years. Both sorts of losses can be deducted from capital gains, but where a gain is exempt from tax a loss on the same asset is not allowable. In calculating taxable gains, the first step is to deduct allowable losses for the same year, and if the resultant net amount exceeds the 'annual exempt amount' you can then deduct any carried forward losses from previous years that you might have.

Indexation allowance

Indexation allowance (IA) is the allowance that adjusts gains for the effects of inflation. Its importance has been severely curtailed by the Finance Act 1998, which introduced 'taper relief' and froze the IA at 5 April 1998, making the allowance available only for periods preceding 31 March 1998. To calculate IA up to April 1998, the taxpayer consults tables provided by the IR that give the indexation factor by which the gross gain is multiplied. For assets held on 5 April 1998 both IA and taper relief will apply on disposal.

Deductions

The costs of acquisition, enhancement and disposal of an asset can be deducted from the gain. Also, the cost of defending your right to ownership of the asset can be deducted, whilst the normal cost of repairs and maintenance and interest payments cannot. Special rules apply to the costs of 'wasting assets' (which are defined as assets which had a predictable life of less than 50 years when acquired).

Acquisition costs are defined as being costs wholly and exclusively incurred in acquiring the asset. Where the asset is business goodwill, any capital costs expressly incurred wholly and exclusively in creating the asset can be deducted.

Enhancement costs are those costs wholly and exclusively incurred to enhance the asset as long as the costs are still reflected in the nature of the asset at the date of sale.

Incidental costs include costs of transfer or conveyance; and fees, commissions and remuneration for professional advice.

RELIEFS (OTHER THAN TAPER RELIEF)

Reliefs come in various forms. Some defer charges, whilst others reduce the amount of tax before taper relief is applied. Some are allowed automatically, whilst others have to be claimed before the IR will allow them. The more important reliefs as far as business owners are concerned are as follows:

Rollover relief (also sometimes called holdover relief)

Rollover relief allows gains on disposal of business assets (excluding shares) to be deferred if you purchase replacement business assets with the proceeds. 'Share for share' exchanges can be eligible for holdover relief, which results in the CGT being deferred until the second parcel of shares is sold.

Retirement relief

This relief was phased out in April 2003.

Special investments

If you dispose of shares in a business in which you were either receiving the Enterprise Investment Scheme income tax relief, or which is a nominated Venture Capital Trust, your gains are exempt if you meet certain qualifying conditions.

Business transfer relief

Where you transfer a business you own to a company you own in exchange for shares, your gains are deferred until you sell the shares.

Gifts hold over relief

This relief allows gains to be deferred when certain assets are given away or sold at less than arm's length value. An example of this would be a sale to a family member at less than fair market value.

TAPER RELIEF

General principles

Business Asset Taper Relief, introduced in the Finance Act 1998, is now the most important relief from CGT as far as private business owners are concerned. Taper relief reduces the proportion of gain chargeable to CGT according to the period of time the asset has been owned by individuals, trustees and personal representatives.

The rate of the taper depends on whether the asset is a business or non-business asset.

a) Rates for business assets

The amount of relief is announced in the Budget and for business assets disposed of after 6 April 2006 is as follows:

After one year qualifying period: 50%

After two years qualifying period: 25%

As you can see, after two years of ownership the percentage of gain that is chargeable will be reduced to 25%. This means that at the top rate of tax CGT will effectively be charged at 10% (that is, 25% of 40%).

b) Rates for non-business assets

Figure 10.1, below shows the percentage of chargeable gain that is applicable to non-business assets.

No. of whole years in qualifying period	Percentage of gain chargeable
1	100%
2	100%
3	95%
4	90%
5	85%
6	80%
7	75%
8	70%
9	65%
10 or more	60%

Figure 10.1. CGT: Non-business assets.

c) Indexation

Taper relief replaced indexation from April 1998, but not for assets held on or before 5 April 1998. This means that both the taper relief and indexation rules will still apply to some asset disposals. (You now know why we need tax advisors!) Taper relief is applied after all other reliefs and allowances have been given, but before the annual exempt amount is applied.

It is important to note that Taper relief is usually available to individuals who own assets and not to companies for whom the indexation allowance will continue to apply.

Important terminology for taper relief

The IR loves technical terms and the important ones to understand in taper relief are as follows:

'Qualifying holding period'

The percentage of gain chargeable depends on 'the number of whole years' in the qualifying holding period, which is simply the relevant period that the asset was owned by the seller. (Note that where an asset is acquired through an option, the qualifying holding period is deemed to be from the exercise of the option and not from the grant or acquisition of the option.)

'Business asset'

Any asset may be a business asset if it is used for the purposes of trade, profession or vocation or employment and if certain conditions are met. The holding of shares is a business asset where the company concerned is a qualifying company.

'Qualifying company'

A qualifying company is a trading company, or the subsidiary or the holding company of a trading company, where the relevant individual can exercise at least 25% of the voting rights in that company; or if it is a trading company and the individual owns at least 5% of the shares in the company and is working fulltime in the company. Difficulties can arise where the holding company has more than one subsidiary, some of which are not trading companies.

'Trade' and 'trading company'

Trade is deemed to be anything that is considered by the IR as trade for the purpose of income tax, and a trading company is a company wholly engaged in trade. (Note that there can be practical difficulties in this definition for some private business owners.)

How to calculate CGT after taper relief

The IR states that the way CGT is calculated is aimed at reducing the amount of CGT payable on each asset by the taxpayer. Whatever the truth of the matter, calculating the CGT can have its own complications (for example, which losses to deduct from which gains?) but, in simple terms, you go about calculating your CGT liability for business assets (that have been business assets for the whole period of ownership) in the following way:

Example 1: Where you have no allowable losses

Step 1: Calculate your gain for the year. (You do this by deducting the cost of the asset, including incidental costs, from the disposal proceeds.)

Step 2: If the asset was owned before 1998, calculate the indexation allowance and deduct this from the gain to get the chargeable gain.

Calculating capital gains tax

This example is for when there are no allowable losses and is based on the relief available in April 2004.

- You acquire a business asset on 10th July 2002 for £150 000 (including incidental costs) and you sell the asset on 8th September 2004 for £265 000.

- Your untapered chargeable gain is therefore £115 000.

- You have no other chargeable gains or allowable losses in the tax year.

- There are two whole years in your qualifying holding period for taper relief purposes.

- The taper relief percentage of gain chargeable for a business asset held for two years is 25%.

Assuming that your exempt amount is £8200, the amount liable to CGT is computed as follows:

1	Total Chargeable gain £115 000 at 25% =	£28 750
2	Less annual exempt amount	£8 500
3	Taxable Amount liable to CGT	£20 250

Figure 10.2. Calculating capital gains tax.

Step 3: Calculate the number of whole years you have owned the asset to work out the taper relief and the resultant tapered chargeable gain.

Step 4: Deduct the annual exempt amount from the tapered chargeable gain to arrive at the 'amount liable to CGT'.

Figure 10.2 above, provides an example of this calculation.

Example 2: Where there are allowable losses
Step 1: Calculate your gain for the year, as in Example 1, Step 1 above.

Step 2: Deduct any allowable losses for the year and any losses brought forward from previous years from your gain. If the net amount is either negative, or is less than the annual exempt amount for the year, you do not have any CGT to pay and there is no taper relief to be calculated.

Step 3: If the chargeable amount exceeds the annual exempt amount for the year you calculate the taper relief applicable to each asset. (This is an example of where it is important that the appropriate losses are deducted from the various assets in the way most favourable for you.)

Step 4: Deduct the annual exempt amount from the tapered chargeable gain to arrive at the amount liable to CGT.

Common pitfalls with taper relief
Certain business owners will not receive full advantage from taper relief due to lack of planning and proper advice. Some of the more common pitfalls are as follows:

- Failing to qualify as a trading company. This can arise because the company owns too high a proportion of its total assets in investments not related to its trading activities, or has minority investments in other companies.
- Unwittingly restarting the taper relief clock. This can arise, for example, where shares are transferred to business associates shortly before the sale of the business to reflect previously agreed shareholding that have not been formally documented, resulting in the taper relief being recalculated from the date of transfer and a resultant loss of the tax benefit for the transferees. Or, if an owner gives away shares or other assets (by putting them into a trust for his children, for example) the clock starts ticking again from the date of the gift.

- Where the shares sold are those of a subsidiary owned by a holding company, the holding company's trading company status (and its eligibility to business asset taper relief) can be lost if there are other subsidiaries in the group that are not trading companies.
- Where business assets attract both non-business and business taper relief it will take ten years of the qualifying holding period (under current taxation rules) to achieve an effective tax rate of 10%, and not two years as for business asset taper relief.

Some further points of note

- One way of receiving the full benefit of taper relief even though the business assets have not been owned for two years, could be to delay payment through instruments like bank guaranteed loan notes (or corporate bonds). These are cashable sometime in the future with the result that CGT could be payable only at the future date when full taper relief could apply, because for CGT purposes the date of disposal is calculated from the date of payment and not when the agreement to sell is entered into. However, you need to be careful that the right kinds of notes have been issued and it is prudent in all cases to receive prior IR clearance.
- Other schemes for avoiding tax include giving up your UK residence and being paid in a qualifying overseas country, because non-UK residents do not pay CGT. However, besides the question of whether the saving is worth this inconvenience, you would need to be careful about how soon you return to the UK and whether this loophole has not been closed.
- Payment of a capital sum over time is still treated as capital (and not income) for CGT purposes, unless something in the sales agreement affects the amount of the selling price.
- Goodwill is a business asset for CGT purposes and is subject to the same rules and allowances and reliefs as other business assets. However, it will be important to both vendor and purchaser to establish clearly what portion, if any, of the price being paid can be allocated to a goodwill component.

How much **CGT** you pay

Once you have calculated the 'amount liable to CGT' you still need to know how much tax to pay the IR. The rate at which CGT is payable depends on the individual taxpayer's income tax rate for the year in question. The amount liable to tax is treated as the 'top slice' of your income (i.e. it is added to your income for the year) and charged to CGT at the rate applicable (sometimes known as the 'marginal rate'). Depending on your total income for the year, the rate could be at the basic rate or the higher rate, or some at the basic rate and the balance at the higher rate.

Establishing your likely **CGT** liability

It is obviously useful if you can estimate in advance what the likely CGT consequences of your asset disposals it will be. You should get expert taxation advice on this and will help if you have kept your business records in an orderly fashion. The checklist in Figure 10.3 below, reminds you of the records you should keep.

As a minimum, you should keep a record of the following facts, so that you are able to get advice from your advisors and clearance, if necessary, from the IR:

- Who is the seller of the assets?
- What is being sold, the company's shares, or the assets of the business?
- The dates you (or the selling entity if this is not you) acquired the assets.
- If the shares in the company are being sold, the date on which the shares were acquired.
- The costs of purchase, including acquisition and likely disposal costs (such as legal fees, commissions, etc.).
- The costs of any additions or enhancements to the assets.
- The estimated date of disposal.
- The estimated price of disposal.
- The likely losses, allowances and reliefs available.
- An estimate of the likely capital gains or losses for each asset.

Figure 10.3. CGT adviser checklist.

INHERITANCE TAX (IHT)

INTRODUCTION

Where a person transfers anything of value either on death or during his lifetime, Inheritance Tax (IHT) may be payable. This fact could have a dramatic impact on the way a business owner structures a family succession plan.

IHT law, like most tax laws, is complex and an understanding of its implications requires careful study. Business owners contemplating a family succession as an exit route should obtain early advice on IHT law from their tax advisors.

GENERAL RULES

- On death the transfer of an estate of a UK resident up to a certain value is tax-free.
- For the tax year 2005/2006 the tax free amount is £275 000.
- Transfers to your spouse of any property either in life or after death, if both spouses are resident in the UK, are also free of tax.
- Gifts can be tax free if certain conditions are met. These conditions include that the transferor lives for seven years after making the gift, or that the gift does not exceed a certain (relatively small) value, or that the total value of gifts does not exceed a specified amount in any single year.
- Besides the exemptions for transfers after death and for gifts made in life, there is also significant business property relief under the IHT legislation, which could be crucial for business owners wishing to dispose of their business assets to family members, either through a sale at less than arm's length, or through a gift, or a combination of both.

BUSINESS PROPERTY RELIEF FROM IHT

This explanation of the relief given on transfers of business property is a very simplified one and expert advice must be taken before you embark on any plans to dispose of your business asset through a gift to family members.

Some of the more important aspects of the business property relief are as follows:

- For the transfer of business assets both in life and on death, relief is available for certain property, known as 'relevant business property', subject to the property having been owned by the transferee for a certain time (usually two years) immediately prior to the transfer.
- The relief available is either 100% or 50% depending on the nature of the business and the property and also whether the transferor has or had 'control' of the business. As a generalisation, the more favourable rate applies to privately owned trading companies.
- Certain companies are not eligible for the relief, including those engaged wholly or mainly in dealing with securities, land and buildings and investments. (A bias similar to the definition of a 'qualifying company' in taper relief for CGT purposes.)
- If the property is an unincorporated business, or an interest in such a business, the value for the purpose of relief is the net value; that is the gross value of assets (including goodwill), less the value of liabilities.
- Where a transferor dies within seven years of a gift of business property, business property relief will be given if:

    1 the property was relevant business property at the time of the transfer, and

    2 it has been owned continuously by the transferor, and

    3 it has remained relevant business property at the time of the transferor's death.

    Relief is reduced in proportion to value if part of the property fails any of these tests.

- Business property relief will remove the issue of whether to taper the relief according to the length of time the transferor has lived after the gift was given by him or her (assuming the time is less than seven years).

(Note: there are similar provisions for the transfer of agricultural assets.)

ESTABLISHING THE FACTS

In a family succession you might decide to transfer your business to an heir for less than market value (for example, as a gift), as this could have several advantages to all concerned. To help you to get advice on the likely IHT consequences of this we provide you with a series of questions in the IHT checklist, Figure 10.4 below.

- What is being transferred: the shares in the company, or the business assets?
- What is the value of the property being transferred?
- If shares are being transferred, is the company of the type to qualify for business property relief?
- Similarly, if assets are being transferred, will they qualify for business property relief?
- How long has the property being transferred been owned by the transferor?
- What are the likely consequences if the transferor dies within seven years of the transfer?

Figure 10.4. IHT checklist.

INCOME AND CORPORATION TAXES

GENERAL PRINCIPLES

Income and corporation taxes are levied on income or profit. In the disposal of a business, proceeds from the sale of trading assets such as stock are included in the trading income of the business for the year in which they are sold and corporation tax might be payable on any profit resulting from the sale.

Income tax could apply to a business vendor in many other areas too numerous to mention in a book such as this. You should, as a part of your exit planning, review with your advisors the likely impact the sale of your business will have on your personal income tax, particularly with regard to the proposed timing of the sale. Early advice will give you the time to plan for the optimum outcomes. Also, it is difficult, and often illegal, to backtrack on transactions after they have been processed, so it is necessary to get it right the first time.

ESTABLISHING THE FACTS

Depending on the structure and nature of the sale and your own circumstances, there are many questions you will need to raise with your advisors to establish the likely taxation consequences of your disposal. Some of these are listed in the checklist in Figure 10. 5 below.

- What is being sold: the company's shares, or the business assets?
- The 'cut off' question: what income and expenditure items are likely to be included in the respective accounts of the vendor and purchaser, assuming the disposal goes ahead on the planned date?
- Is it possible to, and are there advantages to, classify some of the assets that are being sold as capital assets rather than trading assets, and *vice versa*?
- Is there the opportunity, or any advantage, in preserving income and/or capital tax losses within the company? (This will be relevant when you plan to sell the assets of the business and not the company that owns them.)
- What is the position regarding recoupment of depreciation expenses in a sale of the assets in question?
- Does the transaction involve transferring sale proceeds from your company (or trust) to your own hands as shareholder/vendor, and what are the taxation implications of this?

Figure 10.5. Income and corporation tax checklist.

Generally speaking, as corporation tax is paid on profits (i.e. the difference between income and expenditure) the usual question of allowable deductions will arise. Once more, this issue is outside the scope of this book and is something that will be addressed by your accountants when they prepare the tax returns for the year in which the business assets are sold.

THE IMPORTANCE OF TIME AND TIMING

The need to plan is nowhere clearer than in the field of taxation. Planning is about giving yourself time and taking advantage of timing. It should be clear to you that timing your sale has a crucial impact on taxation liabilities, particularly now that taper relief is such a big part of the CGT regime.

You might need time to adjust how shares are owned within your business structure and you might need time to elapse before you can take full taxation advantage of this structure. Also, you might need to give yourself time to arrange your business affairs so that your company qualifies as a trading company.

You should allow yourself sufficient time to receive advice from the IR on the structure of your proposed sale and, perhaps, clearance for a particular method of payment. Finally, you need time to plan to ensure you avoid the last minute panic that unplanned transactions invariably bring.

A FINAL WORD OF CAUTION

Taxation is a vital part of exit planning and you need to consider the taxation implications of your own plan from the earliest possible stages.

This chapter provides a brief overview of extremely complex legislation that undergoes constant change (often to close loopholes that have been exploited by tax advisors). With a relatively new law like the Finance Act 1998 there is a limited amount of case law to support various professional interpretations of the legislation's application. Because of this, and as each business circumstance is different, extreme caution must be exercised when coming to any conclusions from the generalised statements made here.

The comments in this chapter are not to be taken as advice and it is critical that you obtain independent, up to date legal, accounting and taxation advice prior to setting out on a detailed exit strategy.

SUMMARY

This chapter has addressed issues of CGT, IHT and other taxes relating to the sale of a business. Whilst it cannot be considered definitive, this summary should have helped to clarify some of the taxation implications of the disposal of your business.

11

How to design and implement your Master Exit Plan

In this chapter we will show you how to design and implement your Master Exit Plan (MEP).

The first step is to bring together the various exit-specific plans and decisions we have dealt with so far, including:

- Setting your objectives.

- Checking your ownership structure and arrangements between co-owners.

- Deciding on your exit timetable.

- Choosing the optimum exit option (or method).

- Identifying barriers to exit and impediments to sale.

- Putting in place a taxation minimisation strategy.

The next step is to update your operational business plan and to integrate your exit-specific plans into it. All your objectives and plans to achieve these objectives can now be summarised into 'things to do' checklists.

You then arrange and prioritise these checklists into a time chart and produce an MEP in both a narrative and a diagrammatic form. This will provide you with a framework that makes your MEP easy to read and follow.

Finally, we consider some first principles of planning which should assist you in implementing and monitoring your plans.

DESIGNING YOUR MASTER EXIT PLAN (MEP)

THE BEST POSSIBLE BUSINESS

The aims of your exit planning should be to arrange your affairs and to groom your business for sale so that you can maximise your after-tax disposal price. This involves some or all of the following actions:

- Structuring your business arrangements so that you are able to be certain, but flexible about your exit plans.
- Arranging your affairs so that you achieve the maximum taxation advantages on exit.
- Choosing the optimum exit option for your business.
- In family successions, choosing the best successor for the business.
- Creating a profitable, growing business by the time of transfer or sale.
- Disposing of the business at the time, and in the way, you planned.
- Planning your personal affairs so that your exit achieves your overall financial objectives.

We have considered previously in this book the selection of the most suitable vehicle through which to trade, the structuring of your business affairs, the choosing of the optimum exit option and identification and removal of impediments to sale. We have considered the idea of tailoring your business from the beginning with your exit option in mind.

To create the best possible business you will need to have followed all these steps and implemented an exit plan so that, when the time comes to dispose of your business, it should have most of the characteristics shown in the checklist in figure 11.1, below.

At the time of disposal your business should have the following characteristics:

- A consistent and profitable trading history.
- A profit trend that is improving and not declining.
- Gross margins at least equal to the industry average.
- Operations governed and monitored with reference to a professionally produced and realistic business plan that includes financial projections for at least three years.

- A good reputation (and, ideally, a strong position) in its industry.
- No significant debt, especially debt secured by personal assets.
- No long-term lease commitments, including asset and property leases. (In particular, property leases should not extend beyond your proposed disposal date.)
- A strong management team with a range of specialist skills necessary for the continuation of the business after disposal.
- A stable work force, controlled employment costs, and sufficient rewards in place for the retention of management and key personal.
- Fully complying with all industrial regulations and legislative requirements.
- Arrangements and agreements with key customers, suppliers and sub-contractors in order and in writing.
- Agency arrangements (where applicable) in order and in writing.
- Suitable insurance in place with regard to fixed assets, stock, equipment, fixtures and fittings and human resources.
- Modern and efficient plant and machinery (including fully computerised office equipment).
- Up to date business records.
- The appearance and 'feel' of a vibrant, go-ahead and enthusiastic organisation, whose profits are improving, rather than a tired, dispirited business that is on a downward spiral. (This improving trend should be confirmed by the financial projections.)

Figure 11.1. The best possible business.

It is, of course, unlikely that your business will have all the characteristics listed in Figure 11.1 by the time you plan to dispose of it. However, you should aim to achieve as many of them as possible. The more time you allow yourself to plan, the more likely you are to succeed.

A NOTE ON RETIREMENT

Where you are disposing of your business and retiring, you should plan to have built up sufficient wealth (with pensions and investments and the sale proceeds of your business) to retire in comfort and security. To achieve this you will need to establish well in advance how much you need to sell your business interests for and then estimate when they will reach this value. This enables you to set an exit date. I suggest you adopt an integrated approach to your personal financial planning and your business exit planning from an early stage and seek the appropriate expert financial and taxation advice.

GETTING STARTED ON YOUR MEP

The time has come to consider putting together a Master Exit Plan (MEP). With a start-up business this will mean committing to paper the ways in which, over an extended period, you plan to achieve the following:

- Develop your business in a way that will suit the exit option you have chosen (what we call 'tailoring' your business for exit).
- Improve your business's operations, profitability and value for exit (what we call 'grooming' for exit).

With a mature business, the emphasis of your MEP will be on grooming it over the period necessary to achieve your exit aims, as it is unlikely that you have already tailored your business over the longer term with its exit option in mind.

But, with all this information and all these aims, targets and jargon you can be excused if you are uncertain where to start!

So, let us take it from the beginning and create a checklist of things to do. Once you have got to grips with the overall task, I will take you through how you put the plan down on paper. I will begin with a start-up business.

Start-up (or early stage) business

This is the ideal time to start your exit planning as you are working with a clean slate and, hopefully, with enthusiastic, co-operative co-owners. At this stage you can make plans to both tailor and groom your business for a successful exit.

A summary of the steps you need to take in designing an MEP for a start-up business is shown in Figure 11.2, below.

1   Confirm and write down your business objectives – see Chapter 1.
2   Decide how you are going to trade (i.e. as a sole trader, or a limited company, etc.) after taking appropriate advice, including taxation advice – see Chapters 2 and 10.

3   Establish your exit date – see Chapter 3.

4   Consider the pros and cons of having co-owners – see Chapter 4.

5   Where you have co-owners, enter into a shareholders' agreement and investigate funding the purchase options – see Chapter 5.

6   Establish your likely exit option – see Chapters 6 and 7.

7   At this early stage, your business should not have any impediments to sale, but refer to Chapter 8 for some ideas on what problems and barriers to exit to avoid.

8   Produce a business plan; or where you have one, review and update it.

9   You are now ready to design an MEP, which will enable you to tailor and groom your business with your chosen exit option in mind – see Chapter 9.

Figure 11.2. MEP checklist: start-up business.

A mature business

The steps that a mature business should take to design its MEP are a little different from those that a start-up would take. The main differences will be that you have already made several decisions and developed your business along an established path. The slate is not necessarily clean and you might have to change, or reverse certain actions, whilst other actions (for example, entering into a shareholders' agreement with reluctant co-owners) might not be easy to implement.

A summary of the steps a mature business will need to take in designing an MEP is shown in Figure 11.3, below.

1   Confirm and write down your business objectives – see Chapter 1.

2   Have your business professionally valued – see Appendix 1.

3   If you are a sole trader, check with your accountant the pros and cons of incorporation – see Chapter 2.

4   Establish your exit date – see Chapter 3.

5   Where you have co-owners either enter into a shareholders' agreement, or where you already have one, check that it includes the important provisions I mention in Chapter 5.

6   Establish your optimum exit option – see Chapters 6 and 7.

7   Review your business for its barriers to exit and impediments to sale. If necessary, get expert help on this: see Chapter 8.

8   Get expert taxation advice on your optimum tax strategy both before and after exit – see Chapter 10.

9   Review and update your operational business plan; or where you do not have one, draw up a business plan.

10 You are now ready to design an MEP to enable you to groom your business for exit.

Figure 11.3. MEP checklist: mature business.

Some comments on the summary steps

Choosing your time frame

For the owners of a start-up business an exit date will seem rather remote and you should not try to be too precise on this. Think about it in more general terms: do you aim to exit in five, 10, 15, or 20 years?

With a mature business you need to decide whether to embark on a short-, medium- or a long-term exit plan and to set your target exit date. This will set the parameters of your planning and the extent to which you are able to implement operational improvements, removal of impediments to sale and personal financial planning.

The timing decision enables you to set up an initial time chart, from which you will design your MEP. I consider this more fully in 'Designing your MEP', below.

Where you are a minority shareholder, consider whether you have any power to establish an exit timeframe, or are you entirely dependent on the majority shareholder?

Choosing your exit option

Although the timing of your exit can be decided for you (by ill heath, for example) and the timing could influence the choice of option, you might wish to choose the optimum exit option first and then set your timetable. In some cases, the choice of exit option will fix a minimum time frame. For example, it could take only two years to prepare a business for a trade sale, but it will certainly take at least five years to prepare an heir for a family succession.

Having your business valued

It is difficult to value start-up businesses, because they lack a financial history against which to test their financial projections, so there is little point in obtaining a valuation of a start-up business for exit planning purposes. You could, however, get an opinion, or an estimate as to what your business could be worth at various future dates, if projections are met, to form some initial views on possible exit dates.

It is important for an owner of a mature business who is considering exit in the next five years to obtain both the current value of the business and *realistic* projected future valuations (assuming your operating objectives are achieved) from an expert.

DESIGNING YOUR MEP

Having completed your checklist and gathered your thoughts, you are now ready to progress to the next stage of collating and prioritising the various things you need to do. But before we get on to this, I wish to consider your operational business plan.

Producing an operational business plan

There are, of course, many different ways of writing business plans (and a whole publishing industry devoted almost entirely to the task of explaining how it should be done!). I am assuming that you understand this process and, indeed, already have an operating business plan in place. If you would like to find out more on how to produce a business plan, I suggest you refer to the Helpful Reading section in Appendix 4.

Where you already have an operational business plan in your business (that is, a plan that lays down your operating objectives and the ways in which you are going to achieve them), your exit planning steps should be added to this plan to produce your MEP. Grooming a business can be seen as a way of improving profitability (and value on exit) and in this sense it coincides with the aims of most operational business plans.

When you design an MEP you are adding steps (or things to do) to a business plan, either chronologically before its normal time span (for example, deciding on a trading structure); or chronologically after it (for example, extending the trading targets to an exit date, which could be more than five years hence); or adding exit-specific steps to it (for example, identifying and removing impediments to sale, or drawing up a shareholders' agreement).

Where you currently do not have a business plan, I suggest you think about having one drawn up. An operational business plan is essential in all businesses for reasons almost too numerous to mention and its activities (or things to do) will form a vital part of your MEP.

An operational business plan usually includes a mission statement as a focus for the plan. To get your exit strategy into focus you could include your exit strategy philosophy in the mission statement of your business plan. Figure 11.4, below shows you how this can be done.

An example of a mission statement in a business plan could be:

'Our mission is to be the best high quality widget producer in the UK, ensuring at all times the highest quality of product at competitive prices, whilst providing a stimulating, pleasant workplace for our employees... etc. We plan to exit the business through an MBO to our key management.'

This mission statement can be expanded by including a narrative of more detailed objectives and actions along the following lines:

'I intend to dispose of my business in 2008 through a management buy-out, with my sales manager leading the management team. In this period I need to remove the major impediments to disposal of my business, which I have identified so far to be the following: (*here you would list these impediments*).'

'I intend removing these impediments by the following actions: (*here you would include the 'things to do' necessary to remove the impediments*).'

'I will also need to consult my taxation advisor on the optimum timing of my disposal so that I can be sure of maximising my taxation relief and will adjust my plans subject to his advice.'

'I will need to groom my sales manager to take over as CEO of the business. I believe that she needs to improve her skills in the following areas: (list them) and to achieve this improvement I will provide the following training and assistance: (*here list what you will be doing*).'

Figure 11.4. A note on mission statements.

Collating and prioritising the activities

You are now ready to go into more detail with regard to the activities listed in your MEP Checklist. This involves compiling lists of the things you need to do to prepare your business for disposal and then prioritising these activities.

For example, in the case of the mature business checklist (see Figure 11.3) you could undertake the following:

- Confirm and list the detailed things you need to do to enter into a shareholders' agreement and obtain taxation advice (steps 5 and 8).
- Under Impediments to Sale (step 7) you could take the following action:

  1 Establish what you believe are the structural impediments (or barriers to exit) in your business.
  2 Establish what you believe are the operational impediments to sale in your business.
  3 Decide what steps should be taken to remove these barriers and impediments; in other words, what are the solutions to these problems that you have identified in your business?
  4 Add these solutions (or activities) to your initial time chart list, once you have prioritised them by start date.

- Under business planning (step 9) you could confirm the exit strategy-specific 'things to do' and add them to your time chart list.

By making these lists, you are continuing to build the framework for your MEP. These prioritised activities will be included in your diagrammatic MEP in due course (see Figure 11.6, below). It will probably be necessary to set up schedules (or sub-lists) for the activities under the operational things to do, or removal of impediments to sale, to prevent your chart from becoming too cumbersome.

The MEP overview: time chart

You can set up an easy to follow overview of your MEP by writing down the prioritised activities that you will be undertaking in your exit plan in a simple summary time chart. Put the disposal date at the bottom of the chart and work upwards to the present time.

An initial time chart for a mature business that wishes to exit through an MBO would look something like Figure 11.5, overleaf.

Years to exit	Activity
4	Begin training new managers
	Advertise for new FD
	Obtain CGT advice
	Begin debt reduction programme
	Update business plan – produce operational things to do
	Identify impediments to sale
3	Dispose of loss-making subsidiary
	Dispose of surplus machinery
	Implementation of business plan (see schedule)
	Approach VCs for support of MBO
	Discuss proposition with bank
	Begin removal of impediments to sale (see attached schedule)
2	Confirm CEO-designate
	Appoint lead advisor
	Bring VCs and management team together
	New agency agreements with major suppliers
	Reduce stock levels
	Conduct environmental audit on factory site
	Review personal financial position
	Undertake mock due diligence
1	Dispose of subsidiary surplus to MBO team's requirements
	Further reduce stock
	Finalise VCs' support
	Firm up MBO team's individual financial investments
0	Finalise agreements (see schedule)
	Complete disposal

Figure 11.5. Initial time chart for an MBO.

It is important to be flexible with regard to the timing of completion of activities and the exit itself. Business affairs never work out exactly as planned, so you need to be prepared to adapt to events outside your control, which could be either positive or negative. To allow for the unforeseen, give yourself a time band of about 18 months around your target disposal date.

A detailed MEP Chart

Another way of presenting your overall plan is to set up your MEP in detailed chart form, as shown in Figure 11.6 below.

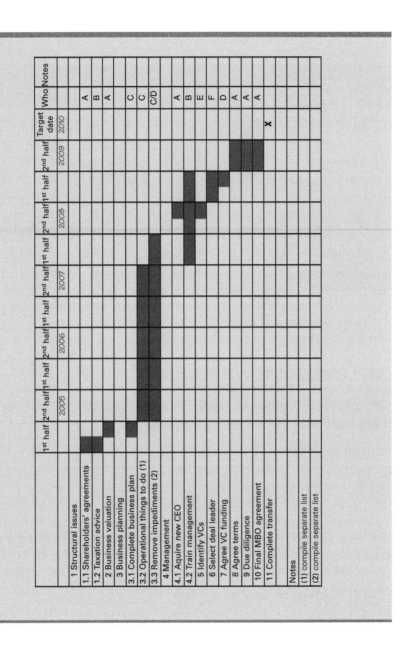

Figure 11.6. Master exit plan: MBO.

To complete the chart, take the following steps:
- Put in disposal date and intervening years. (For your disposal date, rather than setting a specific date, set a band of time of about 18 months in which you plan to dispose of your business.)
- For the current year and, perhaps, the next two years, it is advisable to divide the year up into quarters or halves.
- Working from your summary time chart insert into the diagram the various activities, or 'things to do' that you have identified by working through the steps we have covered so far in this chapter in chronological order of their approximate starting date.
- Estimate how long each activity is likely to take and block out the appropriate time to complete each activity. (Note: it will be easier to move round the activities until you have them in the most logical order of priority if you put the chart on a computer spread sheet. This will also enable you easily to adapt the chart in future if required.)
- Enter the name of the person responsible for undertaking the activity in the appropriate column.

IMPLEMENTING YOUR MEP

You now have a comprehensive MEP both in narrative and chart form and all that remains is for you to implement it!

Unfortunately, despite all the work and expense business owners put into preparing plans, most of them are not implemented properly, if at all. All MEPs will be different in their detail and will have different objectives and 'things to do' and we cannot address all the different issues that could be involved in implementing your particular plan. We can, however, show you how to put systems in place to implement your plans, so that your hard work is not wasted.

YOUR PLANS SHOULD BE REALISTIC

Implementing plans should be a simple matter of doing those things that are included in the 'things to do' section of the plan. This sounds obvious and easy but, as I have said, the reality of business life is that most plans for many reasons are not implemented.

Some of this failure can be put down to incompetent or inadequate execution, but it is also true that some goals are simply not achievable, perhaps because the goals themselves were too optimistic. For example, you might set an objective to increase sales by 15% for each of the next four years, which might seem, in theory to be quite easy. But, if you analyse this more closely, this equates to an increase of nearly 75% in sales over four years. Ask yourself, is this realistic in the light of your sales resources and the state of the market? Also, have you delegated this difficult task to the right people?

SOME SIMPLE PRINCIPLES OF PLANNING

The chances of a plan being implemented will improve if certain simple guidelines are followed at the time the plan is produced. These include the following:

- Ensure that the plans are produced with the involvement of those charged with implementing them. Do not have plans produced by theorists at staff level and expect them to be implemented by line managers.
- Ensure that when the plans are made thought is given to their implementation, with particular regard to the resources in the business.
- Ensure that key managers are committed to the plans and that they confirm their belief that they can be implemented.
- Ensure that the plans are realistic.

One way of checking whether your plans are achievable is for them to be benchmarked against your competition and your industry. Establish what you believe are the key drivers in your business. Now research key financial ratios and performance indicators (from the public sources of financial and company information, such as *Dun and Bradstreet*) to confirm that your plans are realistic in relation to your industry sector and with regard to your own resources: if these are both positive, you should be able to achieve your objectives if your implementation is adequate.

INSTALLING SYSTEMS

Having set sensible, realistic objectives, you now need to ensure that implementation of your plan is undertaken by competent managers and to install systems that ensure continuous monitoring and review of the plan's progress. The following should assist you in these tasks:

- Ensure that your plan is both in writing and in a chart format. The chart should provide an overview that is easy to follow and to monitor. Bigger businesses might feel the need to utilise computer software programmes to monitor their plan's implementation, particularly specific ones such as a marketing plan.
- In smaller businesses the responsibility for implementing the plan usually falls on the owner. With bigger businesses it is important that managers to whom implementation has been delegated have a clear understanding of completion dates and the power to achieve what is asked of them.
- Install systems that ensure implementation and monitoring of the plan is properly managed. You should allocate the task of monitoring to a committee or a senior manager (if you are not going to do it yourself).
- Set down agreed dates to meet the committee, or senior management to review progress. These meetings could be of two kinds:
  1 A formal check of progress, held every two to three months, when you should compare actual results with planned results and make any necessary changes to the timetable and the goals.
  2 A thorough review, held every 12 months, when you should challenge the assumptions of the whole plan in the light of current business circumstances, and rewrite the plan if necessary.

HAVING THE RIGHT APPROACH AND ATTITUDE

Besides setting up the right systems, having the right approach and attitude will also assist in the successful implementation of your MEP. You could be assisted in this by the following guidelines:

- You should start to implement your plan as early as possible, because improvements to a business always take longer to bring about than you think and the unforeseen can always happen.
- You must be flexible and prepared to change your plan regularly as circumstances dictate but, where possible, changes should be made within the established framework of your plan, subject to the 12-month review.

- Be determined and persistent in implementing your plans, and maintain focus on the end result, which is to exit your business for the best price and with the maximum personal satisfaction.
- Ensure you have a mechanism in place that enables you to review the increases in your business's value (a simple relationship between profitability and value will suffice). This could help in keeping you positive and focused about implementing your plans.
- In a family succession, you should involve your successor in the implementation of the plan at all times. Communication at an early stage solves many issues, and prevents small problems from becoming big ones! You should take the same approach, albeit to a lesser extent, with an owner-managed MBO.

Implementation of your MEP is as important as its production, and the problems with implementation can arise from the way the plans were produced as much as from the shortcomings of those implementing them. Teamwork and commitment within the framework of commercial reality are all important elements in both the production of your plans and in their implementation.

SUMMARY

A lot of this chapter, like most work on planning, is rather dry. No wonder it is not the average business owner's favourite subject!

But planning work is time well spent. It enables you to build a practical framework for producing a Master Exit Plan and systems for implementing it. From my experience, the step from producing plans to actually implementing them is often a step too far for most small businesses owners.

Implementation problems sometimes arise because the plans are produced with outside help, which is not present when implementation needs to be carried out. That is why I believe that those responsible for implementing plans should always be involved in producing them. However, even where they have produced the plans, the people responsible for implementing them often do not have the will, or the know-how to achieve a successful outcome. Hence, I have spent some time in this chapter looking at ways that implementation can be improved.

The last word I will leave to Louis V. Gerstner, CEO of IBM, who said:

> 'Execution (the most unappreciated skill of an effective business leader) is about translating strategies into action programmes and measuring their results. It's detailed, it's complicated and it requires a deep understanding of where the business is today and how far away it is from where it needs to be.'

12
Handover and Payment

In this chapter we consider the concluding steps of the exit process. These include:

- How and when to hand over your business after sale.

- The various ways you can get paid for your business, including vendor finance, retentions, deferred payments and earn-outs.

- Issues associated with the sale, such as warranties and completion accounts.

- The pros and cons of the owner staying on in the business.

INTRODUCTION

If you have followed the planning steps in this book, you should be confident that your business is now prepared for exit. You should have achieved most of the objectives in your Master Exit Plan (including removing impediments to sale) well before you become involved in the actual disposal process. Conversely, if you have not planned early, you could be cleaning up your business at the same time as you are selling it!

If your chosen exit was a trade sale, you will have probably approached a business broker or transfer agent, had the business valued and put on the market. Or, you could have handled the sale yourself. Following a marketing campaign, you should have received and be considering some offers.

If you had planned to sell to your management, the various stages of planning for this will be complete, the funding will have been organised and the sale contract ready for signing.

You are now at the stage when the major issues (such as what is being sold and price) have been agreed, but there are still some important practical issues that need to be considered, such as how you get paid, what sort of handover is required and how long you will agree to stay in the business.

THE HANDOVER PROCESS

THE PRINCIPLES OF HANDING OVER

Although the basic objective of a handover is similar for most disposals, namely the seller familiarising the buyer with the operational issues involved in running the business, there are differences depending on the exit route you have taken. In some exit options, such as a flotation, or franchising there will not be a handover at all because you will probably remain in control of the business. In other cases, the handover itself will vary with the length and nature of due diligence, the provisions dealing with the handover in the sale agreement, the size of the business, the time available and the inclination of the seller to undertake a handover process.

For example, in a family succession a handover could be indistinguishable from the training and grooming of the successor and will be for a long period and will largely have taken place before the sale contract has been signed; whereas in a trade sale the handover period will be shorter and will occur mainly after completion of the sale. The handover to internal management in a planned MBO will usually be longer and more extensive than in a venture capitalist-backed MBI. In a merger, the handover could almost be continuous as both sides develop methods of working together over a long period. Finally, a public listing should require no formal handover at all, as the owners of the company that has been listed will usually remain in control after the flotation has been completed.

These differences aside, the general principles of a handover to new owners are shown in Figure 12.1, below.

- In all disposals (except where the vendor is remaining in the business) there needs to be a formal handover of the business by seller to buyer.
- The handover is usually in two parts: the process before completion of the sale, and that after the sale. Although some

people might consider this to be a continuous process, there is a different emphasis in the two processes.

- A handover involves both a handing over of information, and tuition in how things are done. The first is factual, whilst the second could involve certain tricks of the trade, or understanding the personal quirks of employees and customers.

- Before the sale, the emphasis is on the seller explaining the business operations to the buyer, and introducing him or her to the business's key managers and employees, customers, agents, suppliers, sub-contractors, etc. The seller still owns the business and, if the sale falls through, this will remain the case. Because of this, certain highly confidential (or market sensitive) matters might not be divulged.

- After the sale, the seller has no reason to hold back any information. Also, the buyer will be finding out for himself what areas he has difficulties with and will be seeking specific guidance from the seller. Of course, the buyer is now in charge and will, probably, be changing the way things are done anyway, so the seller's help will become progressively less important.

- The length, style and type of handover should be covered in some detail in the sales contract. But, even with a formal agreement on how the handover is to take place, intentions are not always fulfilled in practice because both sides often become disenchanted with the process. The seller finds it difficult to be involved in a business that is no longer his own, whilst the buyer soon wishes to be left alone to do things his way, without what he now considers to be the interference of the old guard.

Figure 12.1. General principles of a handover.

WHEN TO HAND OVER

A handover can be substantially completed before a business sale is finalised. This could happen when the potential buyer has made a final offer, subject only to knowing more about the inner workings and operations of the business. This requirement may not be satisfied by the buyer's formal due diligence process, because this focuses on accounting, legal and compliance issues, rather than operational and managerial issues.

This pre-sale handover provides a difficult challenge to business vendors, because many find it difficult to know just how much they should be telling a potential but, as yet, legally uncommitted buyer about their business.

There is, unfortunately, no easy answer to this dilemma, which relies on a judgement by the seller of the genuineness of the purchaser. The decision you need to make is whether you are involved in a handover of information to a genuine purchaser, or satisfying the curiosity of a potential competitor. If you are in any doubt you should hold back on sensitive information until you have a signed contract, even if it is conditional.

ADVANTAGES OF A PROPER HANDOVER

The handover period is not just to provide information to the buyer, because during this time both buyer and seller are trying to achieve other things. These could include:

- Reassuring management and employees about the future of the business and their role in it.
- Providing comfort to customers or clients that they will continue to receive personal service from the new owner (whom they have now met).
- Establishing buyer relationships with key suppliers.
- Demonstrating to clients and customers that the retiring owner cares about personal relationships, thus helping to preserve client goodwill for the buyer.
- Enabling the seller to leave the business with his relationships and reputation intact, which is especially important in small communities.
- Providing the springboard for the buyer to develop new business opportunities with clients and customers.

SALES CONTRACTS

The disposal transaction will vary depending on the exit route you have chosen. Some aspects, such as due diligence will, however, be more or less the same. In all transactions there will be some form of sales contract. In trade sales, for example, sales contracts are broadly of two kinds, namely:

a) in smaller businesses, those drawn up by the owners or their accountants

b) in most other cases, contracts drawn up by solicitors.

In a trade sale, we believe that it is necessary to use a solicitor to draw up most contracts, except in the case of very small businesses. In other transactions, such as an MBO, it is essential that expert solicitors be used. Where funding is required, lenders or VCs will usually use documentation drawn up by their own solicitors.

GETTING PAID

VENDOR FINANCE (I.E. AGREEING TO BE PAID ON TERMS)

In a trade sale of a smaller business in particular, the seller's willingness to lend the purchaser part of the purchase price can be an extremely useful way to ensure that the seller achieves the price he is looking for. Owners often do not adopt this strategy, largely because they are concerned about not getting paid, or because they need the full proceeds of the sale for some other business purpose, or to retire.

Vendor finance can be particularly useful where the potential buyer shows strong interest in the business and says he would pay the full asking price if he could raise the money, but is short by a specified amount (say £100 000). If the seller does not urgently require the cash, there is a strong argument for considering offering these terms.

In most MBOs, funding is a central issue. Even where MBOs are supported by outside investors (as most of them are) it is my experience that the amount that can be borrowed from banks and financial institutions often falls short of what is required to complete the purchase. Again, the willingness of the vendor to provide funds on terms could be the difference between a deal being completed or not.

But, before you make any decision to provide vendor finance, you should consider the issue carefully. Figure 12.2, below lists some of the questions you should ask yourself.

* Is the sale to my advantage and on terms that are attractive to me?
* Is the fact that the buyer cannot raise the funds likely to kill the deal? (And is there likely to be another buyer who will pay full price without requiring vendor finance?)

- Is the buyer unable to obtain the shortfall from conventional lending sources?
- Can I, for the time being, do without the extra capital I am required to lend to the purchaser?
- Is the interest I can get from the buyer equal to, or better than, the return I could get from investing the sale proceeds elsewhere?
- What is my risk in lending this money? (This can usually be answered by asking what security you are being offered.)
- Am I remaining in the business in some capacity and will this enable me to monitor the business's progress and, hence, my risk?

Figure 12.2. Can I afford vendor finance?

RETENTION OF PART OF THE PURCHASE PRICE

A retention of part of the purchase price usually arises where there is a concern by the buyer that he will not retain certain key clients or customers (or not retain an agreed overall annual sales value of clients) and that this will, consequently, reduce the business's profitability.

For example, the purchaser could agree to buy the business subject to a retention of a part of the purchase price for a minimum of twelve months, with the funds to be held in trust by his solicitor for this period. These monies would be released to the seller if sales (or turnover) targets are achieved, or released *pro rata* if they are only partly achieved.

As a seller you must think carefully before agreeing to a retention. Some of the questions you should ask yourself are listed in Figure 12.3, below.

- Is agreement to the retention necessary to complete the sale?
- Is this the best deal I can get? In other words, could I do an equivalent deal with another buyer, who does not require a retention?
- Is it reasonable to calculate value for my business based on current gross turnover and, therefore, a retention of clients?
- Would it be fairer to base a retention on an overall level of maintainable sales rather than specific key clients (because new clients could compensate for the loss of key clients during the year)?
- How likely is it, in practice, that the business will lose clients and is agreeing to a retention a risk worth taking?

- Does not the retention or otherwise of key clients rely largely on the abilities of the purchaser and why should I be carrying this risk?
- Finally, am I confident that the new owner will be able to maintain the minimum agreed sales figures through his own marketing and sales efforts?

Figure 12.3. Is a retention a good idea?

DEFERRED PAYMENTS

Deferred payment, or payment on terms, could be advantageous for the seller for all sorts of reasons, although it is likely that taxation will be the main reason why a seller could consider it. The potential taxation advantages of being paid over time need to be compared with the risk of not being paid in full; the pros and cons could be very similar to those for vendor finance. You would need expert advice as to how your payments are likely to be treated by the taxation authorities (for example, as income or capital?) before you make any firm decisions in this area.

Loan notes are a way of delaying the receipt of consideration. The issues you need to consider are the date of redemption, whether the payment is guaranteed (and the strength of the guarantee) and the rate and frequency of interest payments. This is a complex area and you should obtain expert taxation advice before agreeing to receive any payment in this way. (Loan notes are covered in more detail in Chapter 10.)

'EARN-OUTS'

This matter has been covered in Chapter 6, but it is worth repeating that where you are selling a business whose asking price is based on predictions of strong growth (and which has little or no hard assets), insistence on an earn-out provision from purchasers is not unusual, and acceptance by you of this arrangement might be the only way you will achieve a sale at the price you are looking for.

RECEIVING SHARES AS CONSIDERATION

With a sale to a plc it is not unusual to be offered some (or all) of the purchase consideration in shares of the purchasing company. Accepting the shares instead of insisting on a cash payment could mean you receive a higher notional purchase price based on the value of the shares on the day the agreement is reached. But, what will the shares be worth when you come to sell them? Of course you hope that they will be worth more, and they might well be, but they could be worth less and, perhaps, even less than the amount you could have received if you had insisted on cash. Also, what sort of return in the form of dividends will you be likely to receive while your money is tied up in the shares?

To help you reach a decision on the risk involved in accepting shares instead of cash you can, if the company is publicly listed, undertake research to discover such things as the company's dividend policy, the volatility of the share price and the liquidity of the shares. Such information is usually not available with private companies, so if you have been offered shares in one as part or full payment for your business you will almost certainly be taking a greater risk.

Generally speaking, shares (especially minority parcels) in a private company are difficult to sell and the ability of minority shareholders to influence such things as dividend policy is limited. Also, the question of what rights attach to the shares being issued to you and how these can be varied will be more transparent in a plc than in a private company.

You need also to be aware that where you are receiving shares in a public company as consideration for some or all of the sale price, there may be a condition in the sales contract which precludes you from selling these shares for some considerable time, possibly up to two years.

TAXATION CONSIDERATIONS

Any arrangements that include deferred or delayed payments of the purchase price of your business, or payment in shares, should be examined by your taxation advisers to ensure you keep your tax liability to a minimum. Deferred payment instruments, such as loan notes, can be a very effective way of reducing your tax liability, but expert advice is required in an area of the law that is always changing.

WARRANTIES AND INDEMNITIES

a) A warranty is an undertaking from a vendor to a purchaser that statements made in the sales contract are correct. (These are usually subject to a 'disclosure undertaking' – see below. An example of a warranty is an undertaking that all litigation with the vendor company has been settled. If these undertakings turn out to be incorrect within a specified time, a penalty will be imposed on the vendor. This penalty is usually a financial one. The total penalties payable can be limited for each individual infringement and/or to a total amount.

A 'disclosure undertaking' is a document that clarifies a general warranty statement. For example, it could state: 'The litigation with Smith and Son, who are claiming a refund on damaged goods of £15000, has yet to be settled.'

b) An indemnity is usually a specific recompense matching a financial loss. For example, if an amount stated to be due to the vendor business from a debtor (say, £50000) is not paid within 24 months of completion of the sale, then the vendor will pay this amount to the purchaser.

Both warranties and indemnities are common in trade sale agreements.

COMPLETION ACCOUNTS

A business's net financial position changes every day. Consequently, where the purchase consideration is based partly on the net asset position, there has to be a 'cut off' date. It is usual for financial statements to be drawn up on the cut off date to finalise the purchase price: these statements are known as 'completion accounts'.

STAYING ON

Many business vendors reaching what is considered to be normal retirement age do not wish to retire completely. They could believe that a sale of their business coupled with a part-time job with the new owner is a perfect way to 'phase themselves out' of business life. Others might feel they cannot afford to retire yet, whilst some will be bound to stay on for a specified period under the sales contract (for example, to maintain client contact). On the other hand, the seller might be staying on, on his insistence, to keep an eye on the business because he has provided vendor finance to the new owners. Because of these various eventualities, it is not unusual for vendors and purchasers to agree that there will be a period in which the vendor will stay on in the business in some capacity or other.

Whatever the reason for staying on, you should be aware that the relationship between a vendor who stays on and the purchaser is seldom a happy one for too long! Many of these arrangements do not last beyond a few months with parties usually delighted when they are brought to a premature end. If staying on after the sale is necessary, it is advisable to keep it as short as possible, unless there are strong personal and contractual reasons why it should be longer.

SUMMARY

I have considered in this chapter various important aspects of a business sale that are often overlooked, or neglected until the last minute. My aim has been to make the business owner aware that:

- There are alternatives to a cash payment for your business, which could have advantages for you.

- How and when a vendor of a small business is paid (or more correctly, is prepared to be paid) can have a large impact on whether or not his business is sold, or whether he achieves his asking price.

- The willingness of the vendor to provide a thorough and lengthy handover can be a telling point in sales negotiations.

- Taxation will be an important issue where deferred payment, or payment other than in cash is being considered.

- Staying on after sale is often traumatic: so keep it as short as possible.

Appendix 1
Valuing your business

In this appendix we examine in some detail the methods employed in valuing private businesses. We will look at:

- Some introductory concepts of valuation, such as real profits, types of value and transferring value.

- Other important issues, such as the concept of risk and a definition of goodwill.

- The commonly accepted methods of valuing private businesses.

- Practical examples of business valuations.

- How you can value your own business.

By reading this appendix you should gain a working knowledge of business valuations that will enable you to form an opinion as to the value of your business. For a formal valuation of your business you should consult an expert valuer.

HOW VALUE CAN INFLUENCE YOUR EXIT PLANS

Having an understanding of the current and future value of your business is vital because:

- It puts your exit planning in its proper context.
- It could influence *when* you exit.
- It influences your post-exit plans including, if applicable, your retirement plans.
- It could affect the way you will implement the operational aspects of your exit planning. For example, how hard you must push to reach a target exit value.

AN ART AND NOT A SCIENCE

Business valuation is an art and not a science, because valuation methods involve subjective judgements of what a business might be worth on the day of valuation, or at some time in the future. From the seller's point of view, the most important valuation opinion is that of a potential purchaser, and no book or article on business valuation is complete without the old chestnut that a business is only worth what a buyer is prepared to pay on the date the seller wishes to sell.

SOME BASIC CONCEPTS

BUSINESS AS AN INVESTMENT

Whatever valuation method is adopted to value a business, it is important for owners to recognise that the valuation should be based on objective criteria (such as are used for the valuation of other investments) and not on subject criteria (including how hard you might have worked on the business to build it up!).

THE ACCEPTED APPROACH

Generally speaking, all accepted business valuation methods place a value on a business by capitalising its expected future profits, or cash flows. However, this approach can be compromised by the fact that the value of the whole business arrived at through these methods can be less than the value of the business's assets based on their market value, or their value in the business's balance sheet.

I will deal with this asset value problem and what is meant by 'capitalisation' later in this appendix.

TRANSFERRING VALUE

A theoretical business value will only become real if the business's assets can be transferred from vendor to purchaser. For example, if the price you ask for your business includes a goodwill value element, you will need to convince the purchaser that the goodwill value can be transferred to him, rather than 'walking out of the door' with you when you leave.

BUYING A BUSINESS OR A COMPANY'S SHARES?

When valuing a business for sale that is operated as a limited company it is necessary to be clear about what is being sold. There are usually two possibilities, namely:

- The sale of the assets of the business (such as stock, plant, fixtures and fittings, debtors, etc.).
- The sale of the company's shares (where usually all assets and most liabilities of the company are transferred).

In the first case you would be valuing assets only (which could include or exclude valuing the goodwill component separately); in the second case you would be valuing a business in total (i.e. the net value of all the assets and liabilities, including any goodwill value, if appropriate).

TYPES OF VALUE

Valuers usually qualify their valuations by stating the circumstances under which the valuation is being undertaken. For example, is the valuation of the business as a 'going concern', or for a close down, or for the sale of assets under duress (i.e. in a 'fire sale')? These circumstances can dramatically affect value as they could determine the presence or otherwise of goodwill value and the price received for individual assets. For example, the value of fixed assets can be greatly reduced in a 'fire sale' when they are moved from their original premises and sold individually, rather than all together as a complete operating unit.

In most cases of exit planning the owners of a business will be considering value as a going concern, but it is useful to be aware of the impact an exit through a close down (particularly a liquidation) could have on your business's value.

'REAL', 'SUPER' AND 'FUTURE MAINTAINABLE' PROFIT

Business value is normally arrived at by capitalising profits (or cash flows). Profits represent the purchaser's return on investment and the reason he is prepared to pay the purchase price. But there are various types of profit, so what do we mean by the term 'profit' and what profit should be used in business valuations?

There are three kinds of profit that you should know about, namely 'real' profit, 'super' profit and 'future maintainable' profit.

Real profit (which is also known as 'adjusted' profit)

The published profit of a private business often gives a distorted view of the real profit of a business. This is because the business owners sometimes arrange matters so as to minimise taxation. On the other hand, some businesses will publish accounts that overstate their profits (or understate their losses) by not including expense items such as rent (where, for example, they own the business premises), or by understating the realistic cost of running the business by not including full salaries for business owners and their families. This can be due to oversight, or an attempt to overstate the value of a business.

In summary, published profits could be different from real profits because:

- Owners mix their private and business financial transactions.
- Profit is shifted between different business entities within the same group.
- In any one year there are non-recurring, or 'one-off' items included in the accounts.

The real profit of a business should be used to arrive at a true value of a business, whatever profit-based valuation method is being used.

Listed below in Figure A1.1 are some of the common adjustments necessary to arrive at real profits for private business.

Non-business items

A private business is a useful vehicle in which non-business expenses can be charged to provide benefit to its owners. Such matters as private motor vehicle, travel and telephone expenses are often included in business expenses and should be eliminated to arrive at real profit.

Non-recurring items

Where a business has any income or expense that is not likely to recur in future this should be removed from the published accounts to arrive at real profit.

Owners' salaries

In calculating real profit it is sometimes necessary to deduct owners' stated salaries from published profits and to replace them with salaries (based on market rates) which would be payable to managers undertaking equivalent work to the owners. Simply, you could ask what the business would need to pay on the open market for managers to undertake the owners' current management tasks.

This is also a useful guideline for an investor/purchaser who does not intend working in the business, as real profit can be calculated for the circumstances where an employed manager will be running the business.

Premises

Where the business owns the premises in which it operates, ownership can reside in different legal entities controlled by the business owner. In these circumstances rental is sometimes completely excluded from published business accounts, or charged at excessive amounts to move profits from one business entity to another.

In calculating real profit it is important that a true market rental figure is included in the business's accounts. The true market rent should be easy to establish. Advice can be sought from your local estate agent if you have any doubts.

Cost of goods sold and gross margins

It is easy to manipulate the profit of any entity that purchases goods by adjusting the value of the closing stock in the accounts at period end. A business can achieve continuously increasing published profits merely by increasing the value of its closing stock. Conversely, a business can often eliminate its profit by writing down the value of its closing stock. In calculating real profits, an amount needs to be added to or subtracted from the accounting profit to allow for any unrealistic valuation of stock.

Figure A1.1. Common profit adjustments to arrive at real profits.

'Super profit'

'Super profit' is similar to real profit and is a term used mainly in smaller businesses. Some small business owners express their profit as gross annual profit before deducting their own salaries (or any amount for market-related salaries that should be paid to compensate the owners for the work they undertake in the business). In these cases, super profit is the amount of profit after deduction has been made for these salaries.

For example, if a business's real profits after adjusting for all non-business expenses, but before allowing for owners' market related wages of £80000 is £250000, then the super profits would be £170000. Or, if in another business the profit is also £250 000 per annum, but market related wages for the owners working in this business are £120 000, the super profits would be £130 000.

'Future maintainable' profit (FMP) or future maintainable earnings

The profit figure that is often used in business valuations is often called future maintainable profit (FMP). It includes an element of real profit and, more correctly, could be called future maintainable real (or adjusted) profit.

FMP involves three concepts, namely:

a) The future, which is self-explanatory.

b) Maintainability, which addresses the question of profits continuing at a certain level and the fact that they can be predicted with some certainty.

c) Profit, which, as I have said, is the real, or adjusted profit.

Valuing a business using FMP involves an element of prediction and is, by definition, uncertain. In private business valuations, FMP is usually calculated by averaging a combination of past and projected profits, which is an interesting mixture of certainty and uncertainty. The averaging sometimes involves weighting past profits at a higher value than future ones. (I will discuss FMP below in more detail.)

WHAT IS CAPITALISATION?

I have already mentioned that, generally, to arrive at the value of a small business one capitalises profits. Capitalisation is the simple process by which you multiply the profit by a multiple (or ratio) to arrive at value. The question of what multiple should be used to arrive at a 'true' valuation takes up a good part of this appendix, as it is involved with the concept of risk and return. I cover this in more detail in the section on the Price Earnings Ratio method of valuation, below.

But first we will look at risk.

THE CONCEPT OF RISK

There are many risks involved in buying a business. Below we consider some of the more straightforward and common ones.

Profit or Income risk

Most investment valuations rely partly on estimates of future returns (or future profits). The risk that future returns will not materialise will be greater with some investments than in others. For example, amongst the less risky investments is a cash deposit in a high street bank with a fixed interest return for a set period (and with an undertaking to receive the capital back in full at the end of the period). At the other end of the spectrum, you could invest in shares in a speculative gold mining business, where there is no certainty that you will receive any dividend or income (or, indeed, get your capital back).

The former investment will offer to provide a lower rate of return because it provides a relatively risk-free opportunity both in terms of income and capital. The latter has to offer you a much higher possible rate of return to compensate you for (or, if you like, to tempt you with) the much higher risk involved in both its income earning potential and certainty of a capital return.

Applying this theory to private businesses, it is obvious that some are more risky than others. For example, compare the purchase of a mobile phone shop on a high street (that has a month-to-month lease, and where competitors can open at any time and where technology is changing rapidly), with purchasing an old-established news agency (that is the only one on the high street and has a long lease). Assuming that both businesses have the same current annual profit and the same tangible net asset value, typically the value of the mobile phone shop would be less than the value of the news agency.

The reason for this difference in business value is because of the difference in the risk involved in maintaining the cash flow (or profits) of the respective businesses. When calculating their respective values you would use a lower multiple (or capitalisation rate) of profit for the mobile phone shop than for the news agency. The buyer of the news agency believes he is more likely to maintain profits and for a longer period than if he had bought the phone shop, and is, therefore, prepared to pay a larger capital sum for the news agency.

This brings us to key building blocks in approaching private business valuations, which are:

a) the higher the risk, the lower the multiple, and the lower the price;

b) the lower the risk, the higher the multiple and the higher the price.

(Note: The multiple used to calculate value can also be viewed as indicating the probability (or risk) of future profit *growth* in the subject company. Should the probability of growth be strong, a higher multiple of current profits will be used. This is similar, but not identical to the approach used in risk/return analysis discussed above.)

Capital risk

The risk of maintaining income (and achieving a reasonable return) is not the only risk in purchasing a business. Another is the risk in getting one's money back (as has been mentioned above with the high street bank or the gold mining venture). This risk also arises when you contemplate what might happen to your investment if the subject business closes down.

Where a business has strong tangible assets, such as real property or modern plant and equipment, there is a greater chance of a recovery of capital on close down and disposal than when a business has very few tangible assets. Consequently, (all other things being equal) the capitalisation rate used to value an asset-rich business is usually higher than for an asset-poor business.

Other risks

There are still other risks involved in buying a business. These include the following:

- Retaining key personnel and management, retaining key customers and suppliers, non-complying use of premises and other environmental issues could all be seen as a part of the risk involved in the business's ability to make profits and its ability to grow its profits in the future.
- Businesses face political risk (such as terrorism), and risks that legislation affecting the circumstances under which they trade can

change. Naturally, this will affect future business values and they should be taken into account when valuing a business, especially large ones. However, it is difficult in the private business sector to construct a valuation methodology to satisfactorily take account of these factors.

(Note: Some of these risks would be considered as impediments to sale: see Chapter 8.)

WHAT IS GOODWILL?

The notion of goodwill value is familiar to all business owners, although a precise description might be more difficult. Once we have looked at some definitions, we will tackle the question of valuing goodwill in a business. So, what is goodwill?

Legal definition

Probably the best-known legal definition is by Lord McNaughten in the case of *I.R.C.* v *Muller and Company* (1901) where he defined goodwill in the following way:

'It is a thing very easy to describe, very difficult to define. It is the benefit and advantage of a good name, reputation and connection of a business. It is the attractive force, which brings in custom. It is the one thing which distinguishes an old established business from the new one at its first start.'

This definition recognises that goodwill has the ability to bring in custom and, therefore, has a benefit, or value to a business, but does not go much further than that. You could, perhaps, deduce from this definition that goodwill is the intangible component of a business that enables the business to earn a greater income than could be generated by the net tangible assets alone.

Accounting definition

Accountants, being less philosophical than lawyers, look at goodwill more simply. A short accounting definition of goodwill is as follows: 'Goodwill is the difference between the total value of a business and its net tangible asset value'.

Although this definition does not necessarily make the concept of goodwill any easier for business people to understand, it does make goodwill easier to value, especially after a business has been sold. For example, assume a retail business with three shops is being sold for £300000, (excluding the real property). The value of the fixtures and fittings in the shops is £50000 based on their written-down value and the value of the stock is £175000 valued at cost. The value of goodwill would be: £300000 − (175000 + 50000) = £75000.

Having got some of the basic concepts out of the way, we will now turn to the consideration of some valuation methods.

VALUATION METHODS

The general approach to valuation that we recommend business owners to take is to employ two valuation methods and to compare the results. Your final opinion could, perhaps, be based on the average of these two results. The two methods we suggest that you use are the 'super profits' method and price earnings (P/E) ratio method, which are explained below.

For completeness I will also explain the discounted cash flow and 'industry yardstick' methods.

'THE SUPER PROFITS' METHOD

The super profits method (or more accurately, the super profits plus net assets method) arrives at a total value of a business by calculating the goodwill value and the net asset value separately and then adding the two values together. It is used mainly in smaller private companies.

To calculate the value of a business using this method you take the following steps:

Step 1: Calculate the average super profits for the last three years – which we will call the maintainable super profit (MSP). Do not deduct taxation.

Step 2: Capitalise the MSP by a factor of between 1 and 2 to arrive at goodwill value. The rationale for this is that the goodwill value of a small private business represents one or two years' before-tax MSP of the business.

Step 3: Calculate the value of the net tangible assets of the business. This is achieved by placing a gross current market value on a going-concern basis on all tangible assets, less any liabilities that are being taken over (for example, creditors and borrowings and lease payments owing on the assets).

Step 4: Add the goodwill value to the net tangible asset value to arrive at total value of the business.

Figure A1.2, below, shows how this is done.

Step 1: Assume profits have been as follows (and we apply a simple average without weighting):
2002: £135 000; 2003: £139 000; 2004: £145 000.
MSP = £(135 000 + 139 000 + 145 000) ÷ 3 = £139 666.

Step 2: Goodwill value = £139 666 x1.5 = £209 499 (say £209 500)

Step 3: Assume gross asset value is £255 000 and liabilities are £118 000, therefore NTA value is £137 000

Step 4: Total business value is £209 500 + £137 000

= £346 500

(Note: Where the company's shares are being sold it is assumed that the purchaser is buying all assets and taking over all liabilities.)

Figure A1.2. A practical example of the super profits method.

THE PRICE EARNINGS (P/E) RATIO METHOD

The P/E ratio method is probably the most widely used valuation method for businesses of all sizes, both public and private. This method values a business as a whole by capitalising its future maintainable after-tax real profits to arrive at total value, rather than by valuing goodwill and net assets separately as is done through the super profits approach. Thus, in a P/E ratio method the total value includes goodwill value.

A P/E ratio is a way of expressing the capital value of an investment. If you receive a return of £25 on an investment with a capital value of £200, to calculate the percentage yield you divide the return by the value of the investment and multiply it by 100: (25 ÷ 200 x 100) = 12.5%.

Conversely, if you know the value of the return (£25) and the yield you wish to achieve in an investment (12.5%), you calculate the value you would place on such an investment by multiplying the return (£25) by a

P/E ratio or multiple. The multiple is arrived at by dividing 100 by the percentage yield (12.5). In our example, the P/E ratio would be $100 \div 12.5 = 8$. If the yield you were looking for was 15% your P/E multiple would be 6.66, and so on.

The concept of the P/E ratio method is simple, but there are practical difficulties with private businesses (especially smaller ones) in establishing the future maintainable profit (FMP) and in deciding what P/E ratio to use in each case.

(Note that assets that are not used to generate the business income – known as 'surplus assets' – including such things as business premises, or other real estate owned by the business, are not included in the total business value calculated by using this method.)

Establishing the FMP

This involves two distinct steps, namely:

a) adjusting the published profits to arrive at real profits;

b) deciding what combination of historic real profits and future profits should be used to arrive at the FMP figure.

The process of adjusting published profits in a private business to reach real profits has been discussed above. Deciding on a final FMP figure is more a matter of judgement, but there are some guidelines you can follow:

1 Although a purchaser is buying the future, he is more likely to believe that last year's profits are a closer proxy for FMP than next year's projected profits.

2 It is usual to use a combination of historic and projected data to establish FMP and an average of the last three years' real profits and the next two years' projected profits (if available) is a good starting point.

3 It could be appropriate to weight the figures in favour of the closest historic results.

Establishing the appropriate P/E ratio

Before we look at a practical example of a P/E valuation, it might be helpful to examine some of the issues you need to consider to establish the appropriate P/E ratio for your own business. What you are looking for is a capitalisation rate that truly reflects the profits risk and the growth potential of your business.

a) The rate of inflation

All investment returns, including official interest rates, are influenced in some way by the rate of inflation. So are P/E ratios. In times of high inflation the return on any investment in percentage terms is expected to be high and, consequently, P/E ratios are low, and in times of low inflation P/E ratios are supposed to be generally higher. However, this correlation does not always apply, particularly on the world's stock exchanges, which are often influenced by other considerations. Thankfully for our purposes, the P/E ratios applicable to private businesses and, hence, their values are much more rational and are usually directly influenced by current inflation rates.

b) Alternative investments

The next step in establishing the appropriate P/E ratio for your business is to find out the current returns of various alternative investments and to list them in order of type and risk. This will give you a point of reference to help you make your selection. Below we list some types of investment and their P/E ratios to which you could refer, and we then ask you to consider some other issues that could establish an appropriate P/E.

1 *Relatively risk-free investments* Consider, for example, an interest-bearing cash deposit in a high street bank. Let us assume this pays 6% before tax, or 4.5% after tax. A 4.5% after tax return is equivalent to a P/E ratio of $100 \div 4.5$, or 22. (Note this investment has neither capital gain nor the risk of loss, whereas most businesses do.)

2 *Sale prices for comparable private businesses* Ask a company broker with knowledge of your industry sector what P/E ratios are currently being applied to business of your type and size and, for sake of interest, in some other sectors of the market. (I expect the answer to be somewhere between 4 and 8.)

3 *London Stock Exchange* Find out what P/E ratios are applicable for public companies in your industry sector on the LSE. The *Financial*

Times publishes average P/E ratios for the LSE for a range of sectors. (See below for more on this.)

Now consider your own company. How does it compare with the examples above? But, before you make a final decision, consider two more aspects, namely:

4 *The view of the buyer* Put yourself in a potential buyer's shoes. What would be a reasonable return on investment in this business, given the risk of maintaining income and incurring capital loss? If you think 15% is a reasonable figure, this equates to a P/E ratio of 6.6; if you consider 10% to be reasonable, this equates to a P/E ratio of 10; and so on.

5 *Getting my money back* Another way of looking at this (especially for smaller companies) is to ask: 'How quickly will the investor want to get his money back?' Or, 'How many years of after-tax profit is reasonable to repay the initial investment in this business?'

c) Comparisons with the LSE P/E ratios

It could be instructive to look at P/Es on the London Stock Exchange. In March 2005 examples of P/Es were: Basic Industrial 12.0; General Industrial 18.9; Consumer Goods 17.7; Financial 13.9; Insurance 10.4; I.T. 42.4; whilst the average for the FTSE 100 was 15.0.

The average P/E ratio on the LSE in your industry sector could be a good reference point in deciding on the appropriate P/E ratio for your business. Public company P/E ratios are usually about twice to three times those of larger private company P/E ratios and three to four times those of smaller private businesses.

One also needs to be aware that there are times when stock exchange P/E ratios mirror the 'irrational exuberance' of the times, whilst private company transactions seldom follow this enthusiastic pricing model. In these circumstances (which pertained prior to 2000), the discount for private companies in relation to public companies would be larger.

d) Private company P/E ratios

A good place to start is a review of private company P/Es in the United States as shown in Figure A1.3, below.

A. Dewing in his *Financial Policy of Corporations* (1935) provides the following guidelines to choosing a P/E ratio for private businesses, based on after-tax profits. These multiples were used for companies in the United States some 70 years ago and are applicable to a time of low economic growth. This is, however, a useful guide to P/E ratios for smaller private companies in the United Kingdom, particularly now that inflation is low.

- For old-established business, with large assets and excellent goodwill: a P/E ratio of 10.

- Well-established business, but requiring considerable management skills: P/E ratio of 8.

- Well-established business, but subject to shifts in general economic conditions and products vulnerable to depressions: P/E ratio of 7.

- Business requiring small capital investment, but above average executive ability to manage: P/E ratio of 5.

- Small industrial business, highly competitive, relatively small capital (one which virtually anyone could run): P/E ratio of 4.

- Business which depends on special, often unusual, skills of one, or a group of managers, small capital, highly competitive, high mortality: P/E ratio of 2.

- Personal service businesses, requiring virtually no capital. Owner has special skills and intensive knowledge of business. Earnings reflect his skill and it is questionable whether it can continue without him: P/E ratio of 1.

Figure A1.3. An American view of private company P/Es.

Most business markets around the world have a two-tiered structure with a large variance between private and public company P/E ratios. Private company valuations are, however, still influenced by public company sentiment because of a trickle-down effect to the private business sector. Generally speaking, private company valuations do not fluctuate as much as public company ones, except where a private company is about to be listed on the Stock Exchange when very high multiples can be applied to it if it is in a fashionable business sector.

Various bodies publish indices of historic P/E values. For example, you could refer to the *BDO Stoy Hayward/Thompson Financial* Private Company Price Index, which gives year-on-year P/E ratios for larger private companies.

Flotations of Internet-related, and other high-tech companies in the late 1990s were based on values that obeyed few valuation rules. It was not only that P/E ratios were high but also that in many cases they did not even apply, because the businesses had never made a profit! In these cases the only rule of valuation that applied was to capitalise hopes and expectations. Here we must rely on the forecasting powers of City bankers, which are beyond the comprehension of mere business people.

e) Summary

In the United Kingdom, current (2005) multiples for larger private companies are in the range from 4 to 9, whilst the P/Es for smaller companies range from 2 to 4. If you follow the steps suggested so far, you will probably come up with a figure for your business within this range.

Valuing a business using the P/E ratio method

Having established how to calculate the FMP and to choose the appropriate P/E ratio for your business, we will now look at how to value a business using this method. The steps involved are as follows:

Step 1: Establish the future maintainable profit (FMP) of the business after taxation.

Step 2: Select the appropriate P/E ratio (or capitalisation rate).

Step 3: Multiply the FMP by the P/E ratio multiple selected, to arrive at total business value.

Step 4: Add the value of surplus assets, if any, to arrive at total value.

Step 5: To value the goodwill, subtract the net tangible asset value from the total business value.

(If the total value of the business does not exceed its net tangible asset value there will be no goodwill value. If total value is less than net tangible asset value there is 'negative goodwill value' and it can be assumed that the value of the assets in some other use exceeds the value of the assets in the business itself as a going concern.)

Figure A1.4, below, shows how to value a business using the P/E ratio method, using past profits and ignoring projected profits.

Step 1: (a) Assume real profits over the last four years have been as follows:

2001: £220000; 2002: £235000; 2003: £225000; and 2004: £266000.

(b) We will weight the profit figures favouring the most recent, as follows:

£(220000 x 1) + (235000 x 2) + (225000 x 3) + (266000 x 4) ÷ 10
= £242500

Step 2: Assume an appropriate P/E ratio is 5.

Step 3: Business value is £242500 x 5 = £1 214 500

Step 4: Assume you have no surplus assets, so total value is:

£1 214 500

Figure A1.4. A practical example of the P/E ratio method.

A NOTE ON ASSET VALUES

It is important to be clear about the difference between asset values and business values. The method used in this appendix has been to value a business as a going concern: that is to value a whole collection of assets, tangible and intangible, together as an entity in their current business use. Asset value alone is not the same as business value, because asset value alone can be more or less than the value of the business in which it is currently being used.

If the assets alone are worth more than the total business value, it is worth considering whether the business should sell its assets and close down, or whether some of the assets could be sold and the business continued without them.

A NOTE ON THE VALUE OF SHARES IN PRIVATE COMPANIES

Our approach here has been to value a whole business, or company. If one wished to arrive at the theoretical value of each share in the company, it is obvious that one could divide the total value of the company by the number of shares on issue. However, in private companies this does not necessarily hold true. A minority shareholding (or a minority parcel of shares) in a private company does not always have the same value *pro rata* as the value of the total shareholding.

One of the reasons that private companies are valued on a lower P/E than public companies is because the shares in private companies are not easily sold. (It is said that there is 'a lack of liquidity' in private company shares.) This lack of liquidity is particularly true of a minority shareholding in a private company. Investors are wary of purchasing minority shareholdings in private companies because minorities have little or no power to influence such things as dividend policy and exit strategy, unless there is a shareholders' agreement in place that protects their position.

If you are valuing a private company for the purpose of disposal of a minority interest in the company that will remain private, you need to be aware that a substantial discount will usually apply to less than a 51% holding. A *pro rata* value will usually only apply if you already have a buyer who is prepared to accept a value on this basis (such as may be stipulated in a shareholders' agreement).

THE DISCOUNTED CASH FLOW (DCF) METHOD

The DCF method of valuation differs from those we have discussed in this appendix in that it takes into consideration the present value of money. (An easy way to understand the concept of present value is to recognise that a pound in your pocket today is worth more than the same pound in your pocket next year.) The other main difference is that the DCF method capitalises (or discounts) projected cash flows rather than capitalising past and expected future accounting profits.

Purists in the universities and corporate finance firms claim that the DCF method is the only proper way to arrive at the true value of a business and, strictly speaking, they could be right. The DCF method is used in most public company valuations (and by public companies when assessing the value of their potential acquisitions). Its practical weakness for private business purposes is that it relies on discounting the values of projected (or estimated) future cash flows. All business forecasting is notoriously unreliable, and forecasting for private business is even less certain than for public companies. For this reason alone, we do not recommend that you attempt to place a value on your business using this method.

Should you be considering a public listing, the valuation experts or your sponsoring broker will probably value your business on this basis (and probably in conjunction with at least one other method). Similarly, should the potential buyers of your business include a venture capitalist

(VC) in their ranks, the VC could use the DCF method to value your business.

If you are interested in learning more about the DCF method, most standard financial or valuation textbooks cover the topic. You should also refer to Appendix 4, Helpful reading.

INDUSTRY YARDSTICKS

In very small businesses, short-cut methods of valuation are common. These are often referred to as 'industry yardsticks', 'standard formulae' or 'industry short cut' valuation methods.

These methods usually place a value on a business or firm based on its annual gross sales (or turnover), or gross profits, rather than on accounting net profit or the net present value of cash flows. In some industries a valuation will be based on even more basic data such as weekly sales, or even the number of tables in a restaurant!

These short cut methods are not as haphazard as they may at first appear and can be viewed as merely a different way of expressing value in relationship to real profits, as they are usually used in those businesses where a fairly standard relationship does exist between gross sales, gross profit and net profit. Such businesses include small professional practices or small retail outlets, where total value can be expressed in terms of a multiple of weekly or annual gross sales. For example, some insurance brokers are valued at between one and two times the total annual commissions earned.

Another argument in their favour is that by valuing a business using gross profit, for example, you are not getting bogged down with deciding what is the real net profit of the business; that is having to decide what expenses and drawings should legitimately be included in accounts and what taxation charge to include to arrive at the real net profit.

Also, some purchasers are interested only in adding the gross turnover or gross profits of their acquisitions to their current operations, by merging the businesses and stripping all overheads from the acquired business.

PUTTING A VALUE ON YOUR BUSINESS

The information contained in this appendix should enable you to form an opinion of the current value of your business. If you have produced realistic profit projections for your business, you should also be able to estimate the future value of your business. This will help you to place your exit planning in a realistic context as well as clarifying your decisions as to when to start planning and how long you need to execute your plan.

Where you are going to estimate the value of your business yourself we recommend that you take the following steps:

1 Gather together all the relevant financial information, including historical accounts, profit forecasts and asset values.

2 Value your business using two different methods. You should compare the valuations and, perhaps, average them.

3 If your business is very small, you should compare the valuations with the relevant industry yardstick or standard formula, if one exists.

4 You should compare your valuations with recent market sales of comparable businesses, if available.

Note: You should be aware that your valuation estimation (and comparable market sales) might not strictly apply to your business because of potential risks associated with it or, put more precisely, because of the risk that profits will not be maintained. Also, your business's real value could, in practice, be less than its theoretical value (arrived at using conventional methods) because of its barriers to exit or impediments to sale. We would hope that you will, in time, remove these barriers, but when you undertake your initial valuation estimates, these problems could still be present and you will have to bear them in mind.

USING VALUATION EXPERTS

Valuers providing a formal valuation for your business will require certain minimum information. Figure A1. 5, below, is a checklist that will assist you in providing this information (as well as reminding you what information you need to collect for your own valuations).

You will need to assemble the following information when you are preparing an opinion as to the value of your business. Professional valuers will, as a minimum, also require this information to provide you with a formal valuation.

1. Background information

A short narrative background of the business. (Type of business, date commenced, location, number of employees, number of owners, plus anything else you think is relevant.)

Legal structure of business; company or trust or partnership. Provide diagrammatic structure if necessary.

2. Financials

Full financials (profit and loss and balance sheets) for at least the previous three years of all entities involved in the business.

Profit and loss and cash flow projections for at least two years.

Full debtors' listing.

Stock details.

List of assets – depreciation schedule.

3. Premises details:

a) Location of business, clarify whether city, suburban or country where this is not obvious.
b) Number of branches and locations.
c) Properties owned or leased?
d) Lease details, plus a copy of all leases.
e) Owned property details, including:

Description and estimated value.

Is property to be valued? (If so, the valuer will advise what information is required.)

4. Taxation returns

Where business is sole trader or partnership, taxation returns for the last three years should be provided. Taxation returns are not usually required to value companies.

5. Franchises, licences, etc.

If the business operates under a franchise or licence agreement, or is reliant on agency agreements for its trade, full details of these and copies of the relevant agreements should be provided.

6. Staff details

These should include:

* Management: number and qualifications.
* Technical: number and qualifications.
* Support staff: number and qualifications.

7. Business plan

A recent business plan (with financial projections) will greatly assist any valuer to understand the business, especially its markets and its marketing plans and, hence its growth potential.

8. Other information

All businesses are different and unless a comprehensive business plan is provided, the valuer will usually request further information before completing a formal valuation.

Figure A1.5. Valuation of business checklist.

SUMMARY

All business valuations involve individuals estimating what they think a business is worth (or will be worth) on a particular day, assuming certain circumstances. Valuation is, therefore, not an exact science. However, if you follow the guidelines in this chapter you should be able to have a reasonable idea of what your business is currently worth and a basis on which to estimate what it could be worth in the future.

In planning your exit you need to know with some certainty not only how much your business is worth now, but also what it is likely to be worth when you plan to exit. This puts all your plans in context and helps you decide such things as your likely exit timetable and even your retirement planning.

We started this book by considering the owner's business aims. These will usually include achieving certain target values for the business by the time of exit. Estimates of future value will be based on profit projections, which will rely on certain operating objectives being achieved within the business. Naturally, there will be a degree of uncertainty surrounding future values, especially if your projections are several years ahead. However, it is better to have some parameters and goals to aim at (despite their uncertainty) than merely to soldier on with no idea where you want to go and what you are trying to achieve.

Appendix 2
Franchisees and agents

In this appendix we will look at the special position that franchisees, agents, and licensees (who, for simplicity sake, I will call 'franchisees') find themselves in when they wish to exit their businesses.

We explain:

- That your agency or franchise agreement is vital to establishing whether you own a business or not.

- What your rights could be when you wish to exit and that these rights could determine your choice of exit options.

- The usual routes to exit available to franchisees, with special emphasis on small business mergers.

- What your principal could be doing to facilitate your exit for value from your business.

- The buyer of last resort facility.

INTRODUCTION

Franchisees often ask me: 'What can I do about exiting my business?'

To all of them I say: 'Well, first tell me what your franchise agreement says about your exit rights.'

'Oh,' they usually reply, 'nothing, as far as I remember.' Or, 'I haven't got a clue!'

I think these comments sum up the way most people go into franchising. They are excited and motivated about the earning potential of their new business and focus on what needs to be done to raise the franchise fee, set up the business, get trained and get on and make some money.

Only later do they think: 'Where do I go from here – how am I going to exit and, hopefully, make a capital profit?

This appendix addresses these questions.

THE VALUE OF AN AGENCY OR FRANCHISE

If you are a self-employed agent, or trade under a franchise (or licence), you own a business that has a value to you because you earn an income from it; but does it also have a capital value? In Appendix 1 I explained that capital value in a business derives from its income (or profits) and that the quantum (or amount) of value is usually arrived at by capitalising estimated future profits by a multiple such as a P/E ratio. I explained, also, that for there to be value for the owner, the business and the income deriving from it has to be capable of being transferred to a third party.

Most franchisees earn income, like any other business, by buying and selling goods and services, but the key difference for franchisees is that they are only able to continue this trade as long as their franchise agreement is in place. Also, their ability to exit the business by selling it on to another owner is subject to their agreement.

DO YOU OWN YOUR BUSINESS?

Assuming your franchise business has the qualities that enable it to be sold for value, two questions still need to be addressed, which are:

* Do you own the business?
* Are you entitled to sell it for value?

The answers to these questions will depend primarily on the terms of the franchise or licence agreement under which you trade and the exit policy that your principal has adopted. (Please note we will use the word 'principal' here to cover the principals of licensees, or franchisees or self-employed agents.)

In the case of most franchise agreements, ownership *per se* is not an issue. It is usually clear that the franchisee owns the franchise business. The exit questions that arise are how, and to whom, is the franchisee able to dispose of his businesses when, and if, he wishes to do so?

With self-employed agents operating under licence the situation is more complicated. In the financial services industry, for example, where self-employed agents provide a professional or financial service or product to clients on behalf of their principals, there is a direct legal relationship between the client and the principal, but not between the client and the agent. The principal is deemed to 'own' the client and the rights to the income generated from the client. The principal bestows certain rights to client income to the agent under the agency agreement, but the agent will usually lose all rights to client income once the agency agreement comes to an end. Furthermore, the agent, on the face of it, has no right to sell the benefit of the client income to another person during the term of his agency.

Although there is no legal right to income or capital benefit to an agent under these circumstances once an agency agreement has terminated, the principals can at their discretion agree that income benefits to the agent will continue after termination, or that income will continue to be paid to his beneficiaries after his death. Similarly, principals can, if they so choose, allow agents to sell their benefits of the income to a third party (usually another agent) for a capital sum, subject to the approval by the principal. All this, if it applies, would be in the franchise or licence agreement, or contained in the principal's exit or succession policy.

FRANCHISE AND AGENCY AGREEMENT (YOUR AGREEMENT)

Your agreement should cover the question of ownership of your franchise business, the ways you are able to dispose of your business, how the business is to be valued on sale and what conditions need to be fulfilled by you and the prospective purchaser before your principal will agree to the transfer.

The value of your business might also be influenced by your agreement, because it could dictate that you are selling in a market controlled by your principal, rather than in one that is free. This could depress your business's sale value. On the other hand, there could be positive factors in your agreement, such as your principal offering funding to purchasers, or themselves offering to buy your business through what is often known as a buyer of last resort (BOLR) facility – see below.

CHECK YOUR AGREEMENT

From what we have said above, it is obvious that the first thing to do if you are a franchisee thinking of selling your business is to check your agreement to see what it says about exit. If it is not clear from the agreement what your principal's policy on exits is, you will need to clarify this with him.

A well thought out exit policy will not only include restrictions on disposal (such as the potential purchaser having to meet certain requirements and be approved by the principal), but should also include guidance and help for franchisees on the question of sale or succession and even provide for the granting of loans on favourable terms to purchasers by the principal.

Unfortunately, in many franchise groups the emphasis is all on selling and starting up franchises with little thought for the franchisee's longer-term future, including their exit rights. Consequently, (particularly with new franchise groups) there is no clear policy laid down, or assistance given, on exit strategy in many franchise agreements and franchisees can be excused for being confused about what exactly they can and cannot do.

The first step towards clarifying your position is to check the existence, or otherwise, of an exit strategy policy within your franchise group.

GROWING YOUR BUSINESS

Growing your business first so that you can sell it later at a profit is a basic part of an exit strategy. One of the biggest motivations for owners in being in business is the ability to realise a reasonable capital sum on disposal (perhaps as a form of retirement plan, or to move on to another, better business); or to be able to pass on a valuable asset to an heir. A progressive, business-like principal will recognise the advantages to you and to its own business of a motivated agent or franchisee who wishes to build a valuable business. From the principal's point of view, the more success their franchisees have the more success they should have.

Business growth can be organic, or it can be through acquisition. In agencies or franchises, acquisition is usually undertaken by acquiring another agency under the same principal, or another franchise under the same franchise system. You should check to see what your principal's policy is on acquisitions and what support, if any, it provides you with to acquire another business within the group. Similarly, you should understand what assistance (for example, managerial or financial) is available from your principal to assist you in organic growth.

There could also be other advantages to your principal if you build your business through acquisitions. In some companies in the insurance industry, for example, if an agent dies or retires, his clients (contained in what is known as a 'client register') revert to the management of the principal and become what are known as 'orphans'. Research has shown that less 'repeat business' is written and there are more lapses with orphans compared with when client registers are transferred to another agent under a managed exit or succession policy.

CHOOSING THE OPTIMUM EXIT OPTION

On the assumption that your agreement allows you some freedom to plan your exit, we will examine the exit options available to agents or franchisees. Most franchises and agencies are small businesses and this fact, together with the fact that they are operated under licence, restricts the choice of disposal options open to them, but there still might be more options available than you are aware of.

Exit options that might be available to franchisees and agents include the following:

- A succession to a family member.
- A management or employee buyout.
- A trade sale.

- A merger with another business.
- A sale to your principal under BOLR.

The first three exit options mentioned above are covered in this book in some detail (see Chapter 6) so we will only cover these briefly, pointing out the differences in approach for agents and franchisees compared with other business structures. We will, however, deal with an exit through a merger in more detail, as it is particularly relevant to smaller businesses. Finally, we will consider sale to the principal through the BOLR facility.

FAMILY SUCCESSION

The only difference here for agents and franchisees could be the restrictions in planning a family succession that are placed on them by their agreement.

It could be possible under the terms of your franchise agreement to pass on your business to an heir in your lifetime. Many principals encourage this option, as the advantages for all are plain to see. If this is allowed by your agreement, you can follow the steps outlined in this book to plan and implement your succession plan.

Some principals will not allow family inheritance of agency businesses during the agent's lifetime, but they will allow the benefit of recurring income to be inherited by nominated next of kin, usually a spouse, when the agent dies. This is, of course, not the same as passing on a whole business, as the next of kin is not permitted to write new business either for existing or new clients. Usually, the principal will take over the new business side of the client base once the agent has died and thus what is inherited is a diminishing income stream with a limited life span. The details of how this works in your particular agency could be of extreme importance to you and you should check your agreement and discuss it with your principal.

A MANAGEMENT OR EMPLOYEE BUYOUT

Many people think that MBOs are reserved for larger businesses and involve venture capitalists and sophisticated financial engineering, but this is not true. An MBO is merely a trade sale where the buyers happen to be your management or employees. Of course, this option is not available to very small franchises and agencies where there is no management structure, but for all other businesses it is an option you should consider.

The reasons why an MBO might be a suitable option for you have been covered in Chapter 6, but it is worthwhile repeating the issues relevant to agencies and franchisees. The advantages of an MBO to franchisees include the following:

a) Your management know your business better than any outside buyer. For example, they will be familiar with the franchise system under which you operate; or, where you are providing personal or financial services as an agent, they will know the clients intimately.

b) You know your own management personally, you understand their strengths and weaknesses (which helps enormously in the grooming and the handover periods) and you should be able to negotiate the buy out in a spirit of positive goodwill.

c) You should be able to structure the sale arrangements to suit your retirement planning needs, including arrangements for continuing to work in the business after its sale if you so wish.

d) As the seller you could derive a great deal of personal satisfaction in seeing people you have worked with and like, taking over a business that has probably been built up through your joint efforts.

A TRADE SALE

Whereas franchisees (especially if they employ senior management) will have various exit options open to them, sole trader agents (especially those without suitable heirs to take over the business) are more limited in their choice. The obvious exit choices for sole traders without heirs are a merger and a trade sale. The problem in a trade sale could be the transference of knowledge of the business because the 'owner is the business' and there is no transition management, so even this option is not necessarily open to sole traders.

A trade sale is covered in Chapter 6, whilst impediments to sale are covered in Chapter 8. You should read these chapters carefully if you are considering a trade sale of your franchise business.

To assist your understanding of the special problems faced by agents and licensees in a trade sale we list below in Figure A2.1 the main points that you need to clarify before you begin to plan a trade sale. The first part concerns issues that should be resolved in your agreement, whilst the second is of a more general nature.

1 Franchise agreement issues

- Does your agreement allow you to sell your business in a trade sale?
- If it does, what restrictions does it place on you? (For example, does your buyer have to be another agent or current franchisee and does the principal have to approve the buyer?)
- Are you allowed to advertise the sale?
- Are you allowed to set the asking price, or is this the preserve of your principal?
- Does your principal provide finance to approved buyers?
- Will your principal provide training to the purchaser? (This will be particularly important if you are unable to stay on after the sale to hand over to the purchaser.)

2 Other issues

- Are you able to assist the purchaser with vendor finance?
- Are you able to stay on and execute a proper handover to the purchaser?
- Is your business so specialised that the purchaser pool is severely restricted?
- Is your business of the sort that the purchaser is likely to find a lender willing to assist with the purchase price?

Figure A2.1. Problems with franchisees in a trade sale.

If you have addressed the issues covered in Figure A2.1 and come up with positive answers, you should be in a position to plan for a trade sale.

A SMALL BUSINESS MERGER

I will now examine in some detail the reasons why a merger could be a useful exit option for franchisees and licensees. Please note that I am talking here about a merger between two very small businesses (often owned and run by a single person with a very small backup staff). These mergers are sometimes known as 'sole trader mergers'.

a) The ingredients of a successful small business merger

A small business merger is often conducted in two stages: the first stage is a merger between the two businesses (with both owners remaining in the combined business), whilst the second stage involves the older owner selling his equity (or the balance of his equity) to the merger partner and, thus, effecting an exit.

The ingredients of a successful small business merger are shown in Figure A2.2, below.

- A business owner (for example a franchisee or licensee) who is planning to exit his business within ten years, who we will call the 'retiring owner', although he or she might wish to exit the business for reasons other than retirement.
- A second sole trader from the same industry, or profession who is at least five to ten years younger than the retiring owner, who we will call the 'acquiring owner'.
- The owners should be personally compatible and have a similar philosophy on the way they do business.
- The acquiring owner must be planning to grow his business, and must believe that acquisition through a merger is a viable growth option.
- Both owners must have a realistic opinion of the fair (or true) market value of their businesses.
- The retiring owner's business should be of a similar size to, or bigger than, the acquiring owner's business. (Where the retiring owner's business is considerably smaller than the acquiring owner's business, a straight trade sale might be a simpler option for both parties.)
- Both owners must be confident of the mutual long-term benefits of the proposed merger.
- The acquiring owner must be comfortable with working with the retiring owner for some time after the merger.

Figure A2.2. The ingredients of a successful small business merger.

b) The steps involved in planning a merger

To plan for the merger you need to take the following steps:

- **Step one**: find a potential merger partner.
- **Step two**: hold initial meetings with the potential merger partner.
- **Step three**: establish the ground rules.
- **Step four**: enter into agreements, namely a merger agreement and a shareholders' or partnership agreement.
- **Step five**: complete the first transfer of your initial equity (and payment, if applicable).
- **Step six**: devise your operational strategy.
- **Step seven**: sell your interests (or balance of your interests).
- **Step eight**: exit.

We will now look at these steps in more detail.

Step one: finding a potential merger partner

As the retiring owner wishing to arrange a small business merger, the first thing you need to do is to confirm that your principal allows such transactions. Once cleared with the principal, locate a younger owner in the same franchise or agency group who is interested in growth through acquisition. Your principal should be able to assist you with this.

Step two: holding initial meetings

Once you have found suitable candidates, you should hold an initial meeting with each of them to explore the possibilities of a merger. These meetings should be informal, although formal undertakings of confidentiality should be exchanged. You should be open about your plans to merge and exchange enough business information to enable both parties to form an initial opinion on the possibilities and opportunities a merger might present. To establish your respective strengths and weaknesses, an informal SWOT analysis of the two businesses could be useful.

Step three: establishing the ground rules

If your initial meeting with any particular potential merger partner has gone well, you should now move on to the next stage of establishing the ground rules for the merger with this potential partner. These ground rules include:

- Establishing the respective values of the businesses.
- Deciding the structure of the merged entity, i.e. partnership or company?
- Agreeing the proposed shareholding in the merged entity. There are at least two ways of approaching this.

    a) The first is to allocate shares strictly on the basis of the respective value of the two businesses. For example, assuming the merged business is a company, if business A is valued at £200000 and business B is valued at £400000, the total value of the merged company is £600000 and A's owner will be allocated one third of the shares in the merged company and B's owner will be allocated two thirds of the shares in the merged company.

    b) The other possibility is that the owners will wish to be equal shareholders from the beginning. This will only work where the acquiring partner has the smaller business, because the retiring owner will not wish to expend cash and increase his business equity relatively close to retirement. The acquiring partner will pay the retiring partner the amount necessary to bring their shareholding to 50% each. This payment is known as the 'equity balancing payment' and when made, represents the first stage of the retiring agent's exit plan.

Step four: entering into agreements

Once you have agreed to the ground rules in principle, the next step is to draw up a merger agreement, and a shareholders' or partnership agreement. It is possible to combine these two agreements into one.

1   The merger agreement

The merger agreement will address the commercial aspects of the merger, including:

- What assets from each business are being merged?
- Into what sort of business entity, for example partnership or company?
- What is the value of these assets?
- What will be the shareholding in the merged entity?

- If shareholding is to be 50:50, and if the respective business assets are not equal in value, how and when will the equity-balancing amount be paid?
- What duties for what monetary return, (e.g. salaries, commission splits, dividends, etc.) will the owners undertake?
- What is the company's policy to be on such things as motor vehicles, business expenses, entertainment, and so on?

2   The shareholders' or partnership agreement

For retiring owners, the shareholders' agreement covers the second stage of their exit plan, namely agreement to buy the balance of their equity. However, the agreement should also govern the circumstances that might lead to the termination of the arrangements between the co-owners and/or the break up of the merged business, and what will happen to the ownership of the shares or interests in these circumstances.

Matters of particular interest in shareholders' agreements for sole trader mergers are the following:

a) For retiring owners, the agreement to purchase their interests on retirement is the culmination of their exit plan.

b) The question of how to treat the potential growth in value of the business while it is a merged entity managed by both owners can be a difficult one. The matters to be considered are as follows:

  - The agreement will usually contain a valuation formula by which the business is to be valued at various times, or on the occurrence of various events. Should the profitability of the business grow, its value will also grow.
  - In the normal course, business owners strive for growth in profitability, because this leads to larger dividend payouts and higher value for their equity. For retiring owners in the merged entity, any growth in value of the business should result in a higher price being paid for the balance of their interests in the businesses.
  - But, acquiring owners have a dilemma: where a valuation formula is included in the agreement, the harder they work to build the merged business's profitability and value, the more

they will have to pay the retiring owners for their shares (although, of course, the acquiring owners' shares will also increase in value proportionally). A compromise needs to be agreed in advance to solve this potential problem.

c) The co-owners in the merged entity will, in most cases, not know each other particularly well and there will be concerns about whether they will be compatible. Because of this it might be wise to include some form of trial period in the agreement, while it is certainly prudent to include provisions that facilitate an easy split up of the merged business in the early stages.

Step five: completing the first transfer (and payment for your initial equity)

You should now receive payment for the initial transfer of equity to the acquiring owner, if a transfer is to take place at this stage – see step seven below for expansion on this.

Step six: devising your operational strategy

You are now in a position to turn your attention to how the business is going to be run, so your next step is to prepare an operational strategy or business plan for the merged business.

During your initial meetings when you were considering the merit in the proposed merger (and when you should have conducted SWOT analyses of the respective businesses) you should have considered in general terms the broad strategy of the merged business. Your planning now concerns both the strategy for the proposed merged entity and the detailed planning issues or 'things to do' of a detailed business plan. You should consider such things as staffing, marketing, premises requirements, financing and operating systems in your plan. The plan should also look beyond the acquiring owner's purchase of the retiring owner's shares to his own exit strategy plan.

Step seven: Sale of your interests

This involves the sale of your interests to the acquiring owner. The sale of your interests can be in stages, or all on your exit. Usually, it is accomplished in two stages as follows:

a) *The initial purchase* There can either be no initial purchase (either because both businesses have the same value, or because the owners are happy to have an unequal shareholding), or there will be an initial purchase to arrive at an equal shareholding. Where this is so, it would constitute step five.

Although the initial purchase will usually be made at the time of the merger, payment for the shares or interests can, by agreement, be made at any time. Indeed, there could be a series of payments over a long period from the acquiring owner to the retiring owner, enabling the retiring owner to progressively quit his equity, and easing the financial burden on the acquiring owner.

b) *The final purchase* This envisages, at the time of retirement, the sale of the balance of the retiring owner's interests to the acquiring owner, thus completing the retiring owner's exit plan under the shareholders' agreement. Again, payment terms can be negotiated to suit both parties.

In the case of the death or critical illness of retiring owners before the planned retirement date, the agreement could either contemplate an immediate transfer of the remaining equity to the acquiring owners and immediate payment to the retiring owners or their estates (particularly if it had been possible to adequately insure the retiring owner for death or critical illness), or immediate transfer of interests but with payment on terms where, perhaps, no funding for the contingency was in place.

Step eight: implementing your exit plan

With agreement to purchase their interests (and, hopefully, funding for most contingencies in place), retiring owners in a small business merger have an almost watertight exit plan in place, whilst acquiring owners have the ability to plan for their acquisition with some certainty. Both parties must realise, however, that there is still a possibility that the plan will not work out entirely as planned.

The practical problems that can occur in these sorts of arrangements include the two owners not working well together in business, or not getting on personally. It is as well to recognise that it may be necessary to unwind the merger and to return to the *status quo*.

c) Practical difficulties in a small business merger

The major problem for retiring owners is to find a suitable merger partner. Having found a potential merger candidate, it is then necessary to overcome the difficulties that can arise with a business marriage where different people have different views on how things should be done. The main differences that need to be overcome if you are to have a successful merged business include the following:

- Different business strategies.
- Different working styles.
- Different business cultures.
- Different attitudes to owners' salaries and benefits.
- Different views on respective business values.

d) Small business merger: the only way out?

Where you are the owner of a very small business with no suitable heirs and no middle management staff, obviously family succession and an MBO are not available to you. You could also have difficulties with a trade sale (because 'you are the business' and could find it difficult to be able to transfer anything of value to a purchaser). Consequently, a merger might be the only viable way of exiting your business for a reasonable price. There are some particular points of note for agents or franchisees who are considering mergers, which are as follows:

- Finding potential merger partners should be relatively easy within your network.
- Your business cultures should be very similar, as you have both been working under the same regulated system.
- The concept of 'mentoring' (where older franchisees train and support younger franchisees) is well established in some networks and it is not a large leap to go from mentoring to working together in a merged entity.
- Some principals strongly favour mergers between franchisees, as questions of approving the purchaser and training new franchisees do not arise with mergers between people already within the group. (Note, however, that other principals have rules against ownership of more than one franchisee business.)
- Principals will usually have more confidence in providing financial

help to an acquiring owner who is already in the group than to an outsider.

BUYER OF LAST RESORT (BOLR) FACILITY

Where principals wish to motivate franchisees or agents to build up a capital value in their businesses and to encourage, or facilitate their exit planning, they could provide a BOLR facility. A BOLR facility is an undertaking by the principal to purchase a business from a franchisee at a certain price, subject to certain conditions. We will now examine briefly how this might apply.

a) The conditions

Usually the BOLR facility will only come into play if the agent has gone through the exit planning steps laid down in the agency agreement to transfer his business and has failed to do so.

b) The price

The BOLR facility is not meant to be a full substitute for a successfully planned exit. The idea is that it is a last resort disposal and the price paid reflects this fact. For example, in businesses with few hard assets, the principal could apply a valuation formula to arrive at a purchase price at a discount of, say, 30% to true market value or, where there is a large asset content in the business, the principal could set the BOLR price at a figure that reflects the market value of net tangible assets only.

c) The existence

The BOLR facility is found only amongst the more enlightened franchise and agency groups. In these groups it has proved to be a highly successful way of underpinning the value of the franchise to franchisees, as well as an effective way of motivating franchisee and agency growth.

SUMMARY

With so many different franchise and agency arrangements in place in the UK, it is impossible to be specific on what particular franchisees and agents can do with regard to their exit planning.

Your agency agreement is everything as far as your rights are concerned and you must start by understanding what you can and cannot do under this agreement.

The need for proper exit planning is becoming increasingly recognised in the franchise industry. You might, however, find that where your principal has not yet developed a policy that fully covers these issues they might be prepared, in consultation with their franchisees, to address the highly important matter of ensuring that you have a significant capital value in your business and that you can realise it on exit. Such a policy is in the interests of both franchisee and principal.

Appendix 3
Exit planning for university spinouts

In this appendix I look at spinout companies set up by universities in the UK to commercialise their research and intellectual property. Talking about spinout success, The Lambert Report (of which more below) concluded:

'The best way to judge quality is by looking at the ability of a spinout to attract external private equity.'

This appendix takes this statement a step further and asks:

- Is a better way to judge the quality of spinouts their ability to provide a return to their investors through a successful exit?
- Are spinouts generally a success when measured in these terms?
- If not, what are the factors that inhibit their success, in other words what are their impediments to a successful exit?
- Which universities are most successful with their spinouts and should the others follow their template?

WHY ARE SPINOUTS SET UP?

In 1998 Prime Minister Tony Blair said:

'Our success depends on how well we exploit our most valuable assets: our knowledge, skills and creativity. These are the key to designing high-value goods and services and advanced business practices. They are at the heart of a modern, knowledge-driven economy.'

Universities and other institutions wishing to commercialise their knowledge, skills and creativity (i.e., their scientific research or inventions) often do so through setting up 'spinout' companies, (or 'spin-offs' as some people call them). Alternatively, the technology can be licensed or sold to existing commercial enterprises.

In UK universities there are currently considerably more spinout companies set up than there are licensing deals, an approach that is becoming increasingly questioned. In the United States, considered the leader in university knowledge transfer, this ratio is reversed.

THE STRUCTURE OF SPINOUTS

University spinout companies are usually set up by academics wishing to commercialise their research, supported by the university where the research has been undertaken. The university will usually own the intellectual property (IP) arising out of the research undertaken by its employed academics.

The university will typically hold its shares through a special purpose company, following the model for spinout companies in the UK laid down in the RSM Robson Rhodes Report: see figure A3.1, below.

Initial 'seed corn' capital to get the business started is usually provided by the university or by government funding through, for example, the Higher Education Innovation Fund. Following this initial funding, the company will attempt to secure further finance from Business Angels and/or venture capitalists (VCs). Consequently, it is usual for spinout companies to have three groups of shareholders, namely the inventor/academics, the university itself and outside investors.

These three groups of shareholders will usually have different business objectives and ambitions and this will, obviously, influence their exit aspirations. The formal relationship between the various groups of shareholders will be governed by a shareholders' agreement produced either by the university or the outside investors.

Sir Christopher Evans, Chairman of Merlin Biosciences and considered to be Britain's most famous biotech entrepreneur said: 'Once created, university spinouts face the same challenges as any other start-up, principally finding finance, attracting and keeping key personnel and delivering on their business models.'

Spinouts also face the same problems in achieving a successful exit as other SMEs; and most of the exit planning issues I have covered in this book will apply equally to them. Where they are different, perhaps, is in the number of times they will seek investment through the various funding 'rounds' that are an integral part of their growth and development. Preparing for each of these funding rounds can be seen as analogous to grooming the business for several exits.

The academics whose discovery or invention is being commercialised usually manage spinouts at start-up. However, many academics find it difficult to handle the extra burden of managing a commercial enterprise and later (perhaps following second round of funding), it is not uncommon for professional, perhaps more commercially-minded, managers to be introduced to the company. The board of directors will usually contain representatives from the company's management, the university and the outside investors.

The RSM Rhodes Robson Report

The Higher Education Funding Council for England (HEFCE) was established in 1992 to administer public funds made available for the provision of teaching and research and related activities in higher education institutions. In 1995 the HEFCE commissioned RSM Robson Rhodes to conduct a study of related companies operating within the higher education sector, and to produce guidance for the sector in the form of recommended practice guidelines.

The report included the following background comments:

- Institutions set up related companies for a variety of reasons. These include: to carry out activities of a commercial nature; to reward, and retain, key academic personnel; to avoid demands on the institution's management resources; or as a means of conducting joint ventures.

- With the increased pressures on funding, institutions are seeking alternative sources of income and are looking to expand their commercial activities. It is likely, therefore, that related companies will play an increasingly significant role within the higher education sector in the future.

- The activities of related companies can vary considerably, including exploitation of the commercial potential from research and intellectual property (IP). They may also help to attract private funders to share in the risks and rewards of ventures which institutions may not otherwise be able to fund.

- By establishing a related company to undertake a commercial activity, an institution may be able to ensure that its powers are not exceeded, that its legal duties (specifically under the law relating to charities) are not breached, and that its governors reduce the risk of personal liability.
- By carrying out activities through a company it may be possible to limit liabilities which may arise, for example through negligence or breach of contract claims.

Figure A3.1: The RSM Rhodes Robson Report

BUSINESS OBJECTIVES

When we consider how spinouts go about their exit planning, it is instructive to consider the differences between them and other small- to medium-sized enterprises (SMEs) about which most of this book has been written. We will begin with business objectives.

A typical SME in the UK will be solely owned, or have co-owners working full time in the business. Some will have outside investors in the form of family members, or perhaps a Business Angel or VC, usually holding a minority interest. In most SMEs the business and exit objectives of co-owners will usually be broadly similar, although the date they wish to exit could be different.

With most spinouts there will be at least three groups of shareholders, namely the inventor/academic, the university and the outside investors, so the individual shareholders will have institutions (whose objectives could be quite different from their own) as fellow shareholders.

THE UNIVERSITY'S OBJECTIVES

Most universities appear to have two major business objectives in setting up spinout companies, namely to enhance the public good through their research and to make money from it. This commercial objective (the 'third stream' of income – after top-up student fees and direct Government funding) is becoming an increasingly significant aspect of university funding and most universities in the UK are keen to develop this side of their business.

To maximise their return from spinouts, universities seek a successful exit. A capital return from a start-up company within a reasonable period presents the best chance of positive return for their investment, as most technology-based start-ups do not generate positive cash flows for many years and are, in fact, very capital-hungry.

THE ACADEMICS' OBJECTIVES

It is more difficult to generalise about the business objectives of academics involved in spinouts. Where the academic becomes the full-time CEO of the business (and effectively leaves his university post), his objectives may well not be similar to those of the typical SME owner (which we considered in Chapter 1). He might, for example, be more interested in preserving a well-paid long-term job than seeking a relatively short-term exit; he might place more emphasis on assisting mankind in general than becoming personally rich; he might consider the business to be his 'baby' and want to hold on to it.

Where the academic's involvement is not full time (for example where professional managers run the business) his objectives could be more like those of an investor, i.e. to achieve the maximum financial return in as short a time as possible, or within a defined time frame.

THE INVESTORS' OBJECTIVES

It is easier to generalise about investors than academics as investor intentions are better documented. Most Business Angels seek an exit within five years, whilst institutional investors seek an exit in five to seven years. Their objectives are normally strictly commercial.

SO HOW ARE THESE OBJECTIVES RECONCILED?

With most spinouts there seems to be, in theory, a consensus on exit objectives when the company is launched. Initial business plans almost always include routine statements such as: 'Exit will be through a trade sale in five years'; or 'Exit will be through a flotation in seven years'. This is aimed at keeping investors happy, but is it what the academics really want? And will they still wish for this outcome in three years' time?

As the business develops, the academic's objectives might change. Business life has its appeal to the CEO of a successful company. But, the power of minority shareholders is limited and exit decisions are usually out of their hands. If the business is successful enough, an exit through either a trade sale or an initial public offering (IPO) – and usually sooner rather than later – will be pushed through by the investors and the university. The investors usually control the business's destiny and they will have ensured they have the final say on exit through the shareholders' agreement, regardless of the personal wishes of the academics – see below.

SHAREHOLDERS' AGREEMENTS

A major component in exit planning for any company with more than one owner is the shareholders' agreement (which we considered in detail in Chapter 7). One of the aims of a well drawn up shareholders' agreement is to ensure that there are no barriers to exit for the majority shareholder. A subsidiary aim could be to protect the rights of minorities in exit.

The original shareholders in spinout companies can go through the process of being involved in more than one shareholders' agreement. The first will be entered into when the company is originally set up (by the academics and the university), whilst the second and subsequent ones could arise when VCs invest in the company.

THE UNIVERSITY SHAREHOLDERS' AGREEMENT

The Robson Rhodes report makes the following comments on the contents of related company shareholders' agreement and Articles, which academics are asked to enter into with the university at start-up:

- 'It would be normal to include pre-emption rights in the share transfer provisions of the joint venture company's Articles of Association, requiring any shareholder wishing to dispose of his shares to offer them to other shareholders first before being entitled to transfer them to a third party.'
- 'A minority shareholder will normally wish to build in certain protections of his position, which go beyond those provided by the general law.'
- 'Is there an exit strategy for the shareholders to realise their shareholding in the company? A majority shareholder will sometimes wish to have the right to require a minority shareholder to

sell his shares if the majority shareholder wishes to sell his shareholding. Equally, a minority shareholder will wish to prevent a majority shareholder from selling unless the majority shareholder procures that any purchaser of its shares also offers to buy out the minority shareholder at the same price per share as it is prepared to pay for the majority holding.'

In practice, from what I have observed, the university shareholders' agreement will contain the following provisions:

- There will be two classes of shareholders, namely the university (through its special purpose company) holding 'A' class shares; and the academic inventors holding 'B' class shares.
- The objects of the company will be something like: 'The business shall be conducted in the best interests of the company on sound commercial principles so as to generate the maximum achievable maintainable profits available for distribution.' – leaving no room for doubt as to why the university, at least, is involved in the enterprise!
- The 'B' class shareholders (who will usually constitute the day-to day management of the company) will require the consent of the 'A' class shareholders before they can commit the company to financial liabilities or commitments above prescribed limits.
- Directors will be appointed to represent each class of shareholder and provision will be made that no business can be conducted at any board meeting unless an 'A' class director is present.
- In the all-important area of share transfers, issues such as pre-emptive rights and transmission on death are usually included either in the agreement or the company's Articles, but most university agreements provide limited protection to minority shareholders (usually the 'B' class/academic shareholders) omitting the 'piggy-back' clause mentioned by Robson Rhodes. Also, the establishment of 'fair value' of shares is usually left to the auditors, a practice that is unsatisfactory in my view, for the reasons I have stated earlier in this book.

THE INVESTOR AGREEMENTS

For many academics the university shareholders' agreement will be the first one they have experienced. However, when the company embarks on second round funding and the VCs produce their agreement, the academics should, in theory, be better equipped to deal with the agreement and, in particular, to negotiate such things as minority protection.

The following points should be noted about investor agreements:

- The investor agreement will seek, above all, to protect the position of the investors. Because investing for profit is their business, it goes without saying that the investors will be intent on maximising their investment through an exit (usually within five to seven years) and will aim to ensure that the agreement facilitates this path.
- Despite the experience of the academics when the second agreement comes around, the process of negotiating the terms of the agreement is usually one-sided: the investors have the money and, accordingly, they have the power.
- With regard to an exit strategy, however, what is good for the investors (and the university) should, in pure monetary terms, be good for the academics also. The only issue of contention could be timing, as the academics might wish to continue in the business for longer than their investor partners.

EXIT OPTIONS AVAILABLE TO SPINOUTS

One of the major pre-requisites for spinouts to receive funding from institutional investors is the successful exit of those investors. In theory, most of the exit options available to SMEs (and discussed in Chapter 6) are available to spinout companies but, in practice, exit in spinouts is confined almost entirely to trade sales and public listings. Why is this?

The first way to answer this question is to ask why exit options other than trade sales or listings are not suitable for spinouts. Looking at them in turn:

- **Family succession**
  This exit is reserved for businesses in which the owner is an individual, with the majority shareholding who has a suitable heir and a business that is conducive to a family succession. Few, if any, spinouts fit this description.
- **Franchising**
  The nature of spinout companies is such that franchising is not a

viable exit option. (Note, however that licensing of technology – somewhat related to franchising – is a common way that universities earn income from inventions or research.)

- **Sole trader merger**
  Spinout companies are not owned by sole traders.
- **Management or employee buy-outs**
  There is no reason why spinout companies cannot be sold to managers and/or employees, but I am not aware of one of any real size or significance that has been exited this way by its original shareholders.

Besides a managed close down (which is not considered as a proper exit by purists) this leaves us with a trade sale and a public listing, or IPO.

THE NUMBER OF SUCCESSFUL EXITS

There are no comprehensive statistics available indicating how many successful exits have been undertaken by university spinouts, or the total amount of money that has been raised from selling equity since the spinout phenomenon began about 30 years ago. However, some information is available that can provide some pointers.

- The majority of the spinout activity is in the major 20 universities in the UK.
- Up to December 2003, these 20 universities are believed to have spun-out about 700 companies in total.
- It is estimated that from 2004 onwards from all UK universities, 300 spinouts will be created each year.
- By December 2003, approximately 20 spinouts had floated on the stock exchange, most of these being from Oxford University, although Cambridge University, Edinburgh University and Imperial College have had some notable successes.
- Although public listings of spinouts are likely to attract the most publicity, a trade sale is a more common exit for spinouts than a public listing.
- Examples of trade sales in the Cambridge Cluster were the acquisition of Adprotech by Canadian Inflazyme Pharmaceuticals

(for an undisclosed sum); Meridica being acquired by Pfizer for £125 million; and Alphamosaic being acquired by Broadcom for £123 million (source the *Library House/Grant Thornton Cambridge Cluster Report 2005*).

- Successful public listings from Oxford University have included Oxford Instruments, Oxford Glycoscience, Oxford Molecular, Powderject Pharmaceuticals, Oxford Biomedical and Oxford Asymmetry.

- Although there are individual success stories (and several academics and investors have made considerable fortunes from spinout companies), anecdotal evidence suggests that only about one in 20 (or 5%) of spinouts has, so far, been a success in the sense of providing a profitable exit for their investors.

- Of course, many more spinout companies have been successful in generating revenues and employment for thousands of people (with several also generating operating profits for their investors) and time will tell whether the successful exit percentage will improve.

IMPEDIMENTS TO SALE

From the statistics above it could be concluded that spinouts have had limited exit success for their investors. To quote a leading academic entrepreneur:

> 'British scientists, particularly those from our universities, have achieved considerable fame for basic discoveries they have made about such things as the nature of matter, the structures of DNA and the shape of the universe. However, they have an equally lamentable reputation for their efforts, or more accurately, their lack of effort, in making a profit from them.'

The Lambert Report stated:

> 'Britain has a world class science base. In terms of productivity and quantity of output it rates fairly highly. But we rate poorly at commercialising that, so the question is what more can be done to make more of the science that comes into the market place?'

Assuming this to be true, what are the factors that inhibit the development of spinout companies, what things reduce their attractiveness to investors or purchasers, thus reducing their saleability and their exit value? Phrased in the terminology of this book, what are their barriers to exit, or impediments to sale?

As Christopher Evans (quoted earlier) has said: 'Once created, university spinouts face the same challenges as any other start-up...' and they will as a group generally have the same impediments to sale as other SMEs. But, from my research I believe that four impediments in particular are present in spinouts. These are:

- Management weakness.
- Protection of intellectual property (IP).
- Access to finance.
- Management/investor relations.

As is always prudent when considering business success or failure, we will begin by looking at the quality of the management.

THE MANAGEMENT OF SPINOUT COMPANIES

Once a spinout has moved past its start-up phase and has secured Business Angel or VC funding, it becomes a collaborative venture between the university and the business world. Does this collaboration work in terms of successful management of the enterprise?

a) The Lambert Report makes the following comments about university management:

- 'Companies and universities are not natural partners: their cultures and their missions are different.'
- '(Academics) ... lack understanding of the rigours of the market place.'
- 'Business is critical of what it sees as the slow moving, bureaucratic and risk-averse style of university management.'

b) Tom Hockaday, Chairman of the University Companies Association, echoed this sentiment when he said:

'Universities still need to invest more in the type of people who have the skills to work at the interface between academia and business.'

c) A prominent venture capitalist has, somewhat less tactfully, recently stated:

'Some academics believe that there is something disreputable in soiling the purity of science by turning it into a money-making enterprise.'

And, addressing both management and IP valuation issues:

'You have to deal with all those academics who do not have a realistic idea of the value of their company or its IP, and then you have to get in proper managers because those academics aren't managers.'

From all these comments it is clear that all is not right with this aspect of spinouts. Lack of management expertise is probably the major impediment to their growth and exit value. It is constructive, therefore to pose the following questions:

- Should academic researchers be involved in managing the commercialisation of their work?
- If so, for how long, at what level and on what basis?
- Is the answer to distance the academics from the strategic and financial management of the company at a fairly early stage and introduce outside professional managers?
- Does the introduction of professional management improve the success rate of spinouts, both with regard to trading performance and exit?

The failure rate for all start-ups is high: they are by nature speculative ventures. Failures in spinouts, unfortunately for their reputation, often receive a great deal of publicity, because they often appear to offer such promise.

A prime example for the failure of excellent science to translate into a successful business enterprise, and one that attracted a great deal of attention, is that of the company that cloned Dolly the sheep. The research to enable the cloning to take place was undertaken by academics at the Roslin Institute near Edinburgh. The ground-breaking techniques were taken up by PPL Therapeutics Limited, resulting in Dolly being cloned in 1996. This gave rise to much comment and debate on the ethics of such activities. However, the company appeared set for a bright future, but it was not to be. By 2002 it began selling off its assets and in 2004 the patent rights to the techniques used to clone animals were sold to USA-based Exeter Life Sciences for the relatively modest sum of £760000. Subsequently, the company has struggled to stave off bankruptcy.

PROTECTING INTELLECTUAL PROPERTY (IP)

There are several problems with the protection of IP in spinouts. The first is the uncertainty that surrounds the question of ownership of IP when university research is carried out in collaboration with a third party. Simply put, who owns the IP, the university or the third party? In the end the decision could rely on the nature of the written collaboration agreement and whether the collaborator is considered to be an agent of the university or not.

This uncertainty over ownership makes negotiations between spinouts and potential investors longer and more expensive than otherwise would be the case, and sometimes prevents investment deals from being completed (and longer-term exit plans coming to fruition).

Probably more worrying for those who set up spinouts is the question of whether they are able to patent their research. This comes down to two separate issues, namely is there any unique property for which a patent will be granted, and has the company itself done anything to prevent it from applying for a patent?

The first part of this question is complex and in the hands of the Patent Office rather than the directors of the spinout company. However, as the case of the researchers into monoclonal antibodies (lead by Cesar Milstein at Cambridge University) shows, the second can be very much influenced by the actions of its inventors. Milstein's team developed the artificial version of natural monoclonal antibodies and were awarded the Nobel Prize in 1984 for their work. Before they patented their research they decided to publish their findings and by this action made it impossible to take out a patent. Once in the public domain, research findings cannot be protected by patent and all the potential commercial advantage of the research was lost.

Blame for these sorts of mistakes is sometimes levelled at the universities' technology transfer offices. Critics point to the variable standard of the management of these offices, saying that many of them provide very little advice or help on what to do about patenting, licence negotiations or marketing of research findings or ideas. However, corporate mistakes are always the ultimate responsibility of the company's management and directors.

LACK OF FUNDING

University spinouts usually start life with 'seed corn' funding from their university, or from the government. Technology companies are cash hungry and their business plans often indicate that they will require repeated injections of capital for several years. So, a spinout needs to able to attract outside investment if it is to survive and prosper.

The first problem for spinouts is to attract the initial round of third party funding. To quote from the Lambert Report:

> 'The quality of spinouts varies widely among different universities. The best way to judge quality is by looking at the ability of a spinout to attract external private equity. This indicates whether there is real market interest in the new company. At one end, Oxford has attracted private capital to 95% of its spinouts since 1997. But almost a third of the universities that created spinouts in 2002 did not bring in external equity for any of their new companies.'

Part of this problem could be the difficulties associated with whether the spinout has any intellectual property that it can patent and the question of who owns the IP, mentioned above. But, assuming the company has secured its patents, another problem for investors is the value of the IP itself. To quote Lambert again:

> 'Universities should adopt a more realistic approach to their IP rights. A lot of VCs believe that universities over-value their IP and put too high a price on it. Universities must realise that generation of IP might cost say £10, but bringing it to market is going to cost you £100 because you have got to develop, market and commercialise it.'

As the VC, quoted above, said: 'You have to deal with all those academics who do not have a realistic idea of the value of their company or its IP ...'

Another challenge for investors is the quality of financial forecasting contained in business plans. If the management of a company are financially and commercial naïve, it highly likely that their business plans will reflect this and investors will be reluctant to invest.

MANAGEMENT/INVESTOR RELATIONS

Once institutional investment has been attracted to the company, the natural source of further funding should be these same institutions. However, to ensure that current investors will commit further funding requires management/investor relations to be sound and investors to have confidence in the management and board of the companies in which they have invested.

From my experience this is an area where academic managers of spinouts fall short. The differences in business and academic cultures that Lambert mentions become more apparent the longer the relationship persists, often leading to a breakdown in trust. This makes it very difficult for spinout managers to attract repeat funding from their investors, particularly when times are tough (and when they most need it!).

The Lambert Report

The *Lambert Review Of Business-University Collaboration*, published in December 2003 looked at the relationship between industry and academia in scientific research and commercialisation of that research.

- It broadly supports the Government's approach to 'third stream funding' which promotes knowledge transfer.
- The amount of money spent by UK companies on research and development (R & D) is low compared with other industrialised nations: about $410 per person compared with $700 per person in France and $1300 in the USA.
- There are barriers to commercialising university IP, including lack of clarity on ownership in research collaboration and in the variable quality of university technology transfer offices.
- Universities perform well by international standards in science and technology. There has been a marked change of culture, with many universities casting off their ivory tower image and playing a much more active role in their regional and national economy.
- But, there had been too much emphasis on spinouts over the last decade compared with licensing (and other forms of

commercialisation).

- Creating spinouts to meet targets is a waste of effort: 'If you want to do a spinout it is easy. You just start up a company and some academic sits around and draws a bit of money from it until the money runs out.'
- Many spinouts fail because they do not attract sufficient outside finance and lack understanding of the rigours of the marketplace. Many of them will go bust because they are not solid enough to attract second-round funding.
- Universities should pursue more licensing deals rather than concentrate on floating more companies. 'There should be a more balanced approach which would include spinouts, but also more effort to build licence fee income with existing businesses ... licensing brings knowledge to the business economy.'
- Some universities have high licensing levels, for example Oxford University has transferred more IP to the market than any other university in this country thanks to high licensing rates.
- Licensing is less resource intensive that spinning out new companies and has a higher probability of getting technology to market ... it has the advantage of using existing expertise rather than building this from scratch.
- There have been spinout successes, but 'it is a mistake for universities to have to set a target for the number of spinouts that should be created, because you may hit the target, but you may not bring benefits.'

Figure A3.2: The Lambert Report

SUMMARY

Spinouts, because of the nature of their assets, the make up of their shareholders and the academic (rather than business) background of their managers, face particular problems in becoming successful enterprises. Some would say that their track record in overcoming these problems has not been good.

The problems we have identified in this appendix centre on capital-raising and achieving a successful exit, and the reasons we have suggested for the problems are lack of management expertise, confusion over the value of IP, inability to attract funding from investor institutions and inability to maintain sound relations with their investors.

Some universities, notably Oxford, Cambridge and Imperial College, appear to have been more successful with their spinouts than others in both capital raising and successful exits (and, probably, by other measures also, such as income and employment generation), but even they appear to lag behind the more successful American universities.

Leaving aside the question of whether spinouts are the optimum way in which to commercialise research (compared with licencing, for example), it appears that more analysis need to be undertaken to determine why spinouts are not as successful as they could be, particularly in realising profit for their investors through successful exits. Furthermore, there could be closer consideration by universities of the following questions:

- Should there be a more rigorous approach to establishing exit planning strategies when spinouts prepare their business plans at start-up?

- Should there be more extensive training of academics intending to commercialise their research in business management and practice, the raising of finance, investor relations, IP protection, marketing and exit planning?

- How can the quality of management and staff in university technology transfer offices be improved?

Also, perhaps those UK universities with a less than successful history with spinouts and those coming into the spinout business for the first time could follow more closely the approach of Oxford and Cambridge Universities, as well as the template established by the successful American academic institutions.

Appendix 4
Helpful reading

The following books and websites contain useful information for the private business owner.

START-UPS

Starting Your Own Business, Jim Green, (How to Books).

How to Set Up and Run Your Own Business, Helen Kogan, (Kogan Page).

Setting up and Running a Limited Company, Robert Browning, (How to Books).

www.businesslink.org This updated site is much improved and covers all stages of small business start-up, growth and development.

www.startups.co.uk Good site with lots of information. My only criticism is that the search facility is not focused enough.

www.smallbusiness.co.uk LloydsTSB Bank site, but worth a visit.

BUSINESS PLANNING

There are hundreds of books on this subject, three of which are:

Preparing a Winning Business Plan, Matthew Record, (How to Books).

The Business Plan Workbook, various authors, (Kogan Page/IOD).

Guide to Business Planning, Friend and Zehle, (Economist Series).

There are also hundreds of websites on business planning.

www.bizplanit.com and **www.businessplans.org** are two good American sites.

www.startups.co.uk and **www.smallbusiness.co.uk** are two good UK sites.

EXIT PLANNING

Exit Strategy Planning: Grooming your business for sale or succession, John Hawkey, (Gower Publishing).

How to Run your Business so you can Leave it in Style, John H. Brown. (BEI – available from **www.exitplanning.com**).

www.exitstrategyplanning.com The website of Buckmaster Hawkey Limited of which the author is a director: provides articles, case studies, opinions and associated information on exit strategy planning.

www.fambiz.com An American site devoted to family business issues, including family succession planning.

www.bizroadmap.com An excellent American small business site covering topics from start-ups to exit planning.

www.exitplanning.com American site: run by John H. Brown. Very good for general approach, but too American-specific for UK readers in such areas as taxation, staff retention, etc.

EXIT OPTIONS

Selling your Business for All it's Worth, Mark Blayney, (How to Books).

The Complete Guide to Selling Your Business, various authors, (Kogan Page/Sunday Times).

Guide to Taking up a Franchise, Barrow, Golzen, Kogan, (Kogan Page).

How to Franchise your Business, Mendolsohn and Acheson, Royal (Bank of Scotland)

The Franchise Bible, Erwin J. Keup (Entrepreneur Press).

Management buy-outs, (Institute of Directors).

Family Business, (Institute of Directors).

www.fambiz.com American site on all aspects of family business, including succession planning.

www.familybizz.net Grant Thornton's site on family business and good for succession planning.

www.bdo.co.uk Go to 'Centre for Family Business' page.

www.franchisebusinesses.co.uk UK-based guide to the franchise market.

www.british-franchise.org.uk The web site for the British Franchise Association containing information for both intending franchisors and franchisees.

www.londonstockexchange.com The LSE provides comprehensive information on listing on both the Main Board and the AIM. It also provides an excellent CD on the listing process.

www.ofex.com Information on how to join OFEX.

www.fsa.gov.uk/ukla The UK Listing Authority's site.

BUSINESS VALUATIONS

The Business Valuation Book, Gabehart and Brinkley, (Amacom).

The Valuation of Business Shares and Other Equity, Wayne Lonegran, (Longmans Professional).

The Small Business Valuation Book, Lawrence Tuller, (Adam).

The Theory Of Financial Decisions, Haley and Schall, (McGraw-Hill).

BUSINESS ORGANISATIONS

www.iod.com The Institute of Directors website.

www.cbi.org.uk The Confederation Of British Industry site. Comprehensive and has an excellent business links page.

www.inst.mgt.org.uk The Institute of Management website.

www.fsb.org.uk the website for the Federation of Small Business.

www.britishchambers.org.uk The British Chambers of Commerce website provides you with contact information for your local Chamber.

GOVERNMENT

www.etrex.com This site provides a list of the web addresses of various associations, groups, government bodies, etc.

www.businesslink.org The updated Businesslink site (which is now excellent) and linked to regional sites throughout England.

www.dti.gov.uk Home page for Department of Trade and Industry.

www.sbs.gov.uk The UK government's Small Business Service website.

For Scotland go to: **www.sbgateway.com**

For Wales go to: **www.businessconnect.org.uk**

For Northern Ireland go to: **www.ednet-ni.com**

www.onlineforbusiness.gov.uk Have a look and decide for yourself what this is all about! Includes information on grants.

www.inlandrevenue.gov.uk/index/htm The Inland revenue website provides a complete resource of information on all taxation issues, most of which can be downloaded free from the site.

www.companies-house.gov.uk The website for Companies House, which provides services and regulates UK companies.

www.open.gov.uk The easy way to find government information and services online.

www.oft.gov.uk The Office of Fair Trading's site.

www.tec.co.uk The Training and Enterprise Council's site.

MISCELLANEOUS

www.igpcorporate.co.uk An excellent on-line facility for incorporating new companies.

www.nfea.com The National Federation of Enterprise Agencies provides support for business start-ups.

FINANCE AND VENTURE CAPITAL

www.bvca.co.uk The website of the British Venture Capital Association.

www.venture-finance.co.uk Venture Capital site of ABN AMRO Bank.

www.nationalbusinessangels.co.uk Information on private funding.

www.ukishelp.co.uk A starting point for discovering what funding is available from the European Union.

www.dti.gov.uk/europe/structural This section of the DTI's site gives you information on the structural funds that are available to SMEs in depressed areas.

www.dti.gov.uk/enterprisegrant Information from the DTI on enterprise grants.

www.businessangels-london.co.uk Provides comprehensive information on how to raise venture capital.

ELECTRONIC NEWSPAPERS

www.ft.com An excellent newspaper site provided by the *Financial Times*.

www.enterprisenetwork.co.uk The website for the *Sunday Times* Enterprise Network.

www.economist.com *The Economist* magazine's website.

www.telegraph.co.uk The electronic *Telegraph*.

Appendix 5
Glossary

COMMON ACRONYMS AND ABBREVIATIONS

BIMBO	Management Buy-in/Buy-out
CEO	Chief Executive Officer
CGT	Capital Gains Tax
EBO	Employee Buy-out
EMIS	Enterprise Management Incentive Scheme
IA	Investor Agreement
IBO	Institutional Buy-out
IHT	Inheritance Tax
IP	Intellectual Property
IPO	Initial Public Offering
IR	Inland Revenue
LSE	London Stock Exchange
MBO	Management Buy-out
MEP	Master Exit Plan
MBI	Management Buy-in
OFEX	Offmarket Exchange
P/E	Price Earnings (ratio)
SHA	Shareholders' Agreement
SME	Small- to Medium-sized Enterprise
VC	Venture Capitalist

Index